Endorsements for Beyond O...

A beautiful book about our beautiful city! In *Beyond Our Efforts*, Mile High Ministries invites us to join them on the journey of justice, mercy, and walking humbly with our God. They lead us down a path of intimacy with God and kingdom action—a well-worn path that they know well.

—ROBERT GELINAS, Colorado Community Church, author of *Finding the Groove: Composing a Jazz-Shaped Faith*

With passion and perspective, *Beyond our Efforts* celebrates what's possible when individuals and communities integrate contemplation and action. Listen to its wisdom; let it inspire and guide you to build a better world.

—PHILEENA HEUERTZ, Gravity: A Center for Contemplative Activism, author of *Mindful Silence: The Heart of Christian Contemplation* and *Pilgrimage of a Soul: Contemplative Spirituality for the Active Life*

Mile High Ministries introduces us to a city, Denver, as liturgy for the seasons. Just as the New Testament begins with a cemetery tour where we meet the founders whose DNA foretold what was to come, *Beyond Our Efforts* takes us to a cemetery to meet Clara Brown and others who shaped the streets and seasons of their city.

This book evokes the spirituality of mystical charismatics who go into communities looking, seeing, and celebrating the signs of the spirit in all parts of the city; where the city is a gift of common grace for everyone, especially the marginalized and forgotten folks. This book celebrates all three persons of the Trinity—Creator, Peacemaker and Transformer—reminding us that we are never more like God than when we live in community and work in collaboration for the spiritual transformation of persons AND the social transformation of places.

Behold, a working biblical theology of place in action and reflection!

—RAY BAKKE, author of *A Theology as Big as the City* and *The Urban Christian*

One year in my Sunday School class we made a model of Nazareth, linking Jesus and cities in my mind, as they have become linked in my life. Still, Jesus' commandment to love God and your neighbor is rather vague. Therefore, I am thrilled that Mile High Ministries has offered a kind of instruction manual in this wonderful book, *Beyond Our Efforts*. I am deeply drawn to the pain, prayers, people, and parties they describe. It is clearly the product of three decades of co-creation, living the neighboring with heart and soul and smart ideas. This book is essential reading for anyone longing to heal our broken society—a book for everyday use as well as profound reflection.

—**MINDY THOMPSON FULLILOVE**, author of *Urban Alchemy: Restoring Joy in America's Sorted-Out Cities.*

My hope is that you find this book if you are one who we lovingly call a contemplative activist—one of those who believe they are "responding to the invitation to participate in God's active love for the poor." Here you will find mentors, spiritual directors, prophets, and artists who open a door to the mystery contained in seeing Jesus in hard places. Here are revelations of tested urban theology, together with rich textures and tapestries of story. The authors from Mile High Ministries open all of this from their sacred place, Denver. Don't miss this one if you are on the pilgrimage; you will find companions here.

—**KIT DANLEY**, Neighborhood Ministries

In a world filled with pain and division, there's a deep need for tangible and practical ways to become peacemakers, for contemplative practices that anchor us and for real life stories that bring hope. Beyond our Efforts embodies this and more. Mile High Ministries has dedicated 30 years to making peace in Denver. As a pastor, leader, and friend, I have witnessed their fruit and benefitted from their leadership and example. The ripples they have made go not only far and wide but deep and lasting, too.

—**KATHY ESCOBAR**, The Refuge, author of *Faith Shift: Finding Your Way Forward When Everything You Believe is Coming Apart*

Every so often you come upon "the real deal." Well this is it! I have witnessed Mile High Ministries firsthand, and they represent what Christianity was meant to be—and on many levels! Read and be excited again.

—**FR. RICHARD ROHR**, Center for Action and Contemplation, author of *Falling Upward: A Spirituality for Two Halves of Life*

Beyond Our Efforts maps a world unseen and gives us a portrait of Denver that is firmer and fuller in its reality than the surface one glimpses with everyday vision. For more than three decades, Mile High Ministries has sowed grace and redemption into some of the city's deepest wounds. *Beyond Our Efforts* envisions an alternative biography to the city we routinely reduce as a backdrop for our own autobiographies.

After reading this book, you'll never look at any city the same.

—**JOHN HAYES,** InnerCHANGE, author of *SubMerge; Living Deep in a Shallow World*

Brace yourself. This is not a book about how to get things done. *Beyond Our Efforts* is an invitation to journey toward a new way of living and seeing; it is a challenge to embrace a posture in our world that leads to inner transformation. This is the more difficult work, and precisely what Mile High Ministries has been teaching by example for thirty years. We cannot miss the importance of this. For it is only when we commit to a journey of transformation within our hearts and minds that peace can flow through us and come to rest on our neighborhoods, communities and the world. This book is a companion for those willing to undergo that journey.

—**MICHAEL HIDALGO,** Denver Community Church, author of *Changing Faith: Questions, Doubts and Choices About the Unchanging God*

A masterpiece of treasures uncovered in the seldom seen landscape of the urban underside. *Beyond Our Efforts* takes readers on a journey into places few venture and fewer still have experienced as sacred. Decades of immersion in the world of struggling humanity have unveiled treasures of wisdom that the Mile High Ministries team now shares with those ready for deeper insights.

—**ROBERT LUPTON,** FCS Urban Ministries, author of *Toxic Charity: How Churches and Charities Hurt Those They Help (and How to Reverse It)*

Simply beautiful! In a mean-spirited age that threatens to make small-hearted cynics of us all, Mile High Ministries courageously lives out the truth of that great line in Dostoyevsky's novel *The Idiot*, "Beauty will save the world." And what could be more beautiful than a community of peacemakers living all four seasons of life in the city they love, like the holy fools that they are? It makes me want to do the same.

—**KRIS ROCKE,** Street Psalms, co-author of *The Geography of Grace: Doing Theology from Below*

Beyond Our Efforts is a must-read for anyone who cares about making a difference where they live. For decades the Mile High Ministries team has led the way when it comes to thoughtful community engagement. I'm grateful and excited that they have gone out of their way to share their wisdom. This book will make you fall in love with both Denver and your own city!

—**DAVE RUNYON,** CityUnite, co-author of *The Art of Neighboring: Building Genuine Relationships Right Outside Your Door*

I love Denver! And I love this book! I was brought to tears as I read of justice heroes and heroines who have shaped Denver since its inception. And riveted to each page as I read about Mile High Ministries learning to see the holiness of God in every corner of this sacred land, even in the most broken people and bloody streets. Thank you, Mile High Ministries, for depicting how you are transforming yourselves and in so doing healing our world.

—**JILL SHOOK,** Missions Door, author of *Making Housing Happen: Faith-based Affordable Housing Models*

My friends at Mile High Ministries have composed a thoughtful and penetrating tapestry of their journey of loving and learning in Christ's name in the city of Denver. It is a testimony of their faithfulness to God's command to care for "the least of these" in our city. The blend of narratives, poetry, and testimonies provide a glimpse into how God can work through faithful servants to bring peace and hope and restoration to others.

—**TED TRAVIS,** Center for Transformational Discipleship, author of *Building Cathedrals: Urban Youth Discipleship That Works*

Since its inception, Mile High Ministries has been cultivating a beautiful mosaic for our city of Denver: intersecting creativity with *shalom,* inviting us all into the flow of their unique story and space in the community. It is no surprise to see their 30th celebration culminate in a book of reflections, prayers, celebrations, stories and art for readers to enjoy. Thank you MHM for being a people who love God and your neighbors, who see beauty waiting to be uncovered, who are willing to dream big dreams, and who dare people of faith to build and share them together.

—**MICHELLE FERRIGNO WARREN,** Christian Community Development Association, author of *The Power of Proximity: Moving Beyond Awareness to Action*

beyond our efforts

THE CENTER FOR URBAN PEACEMAKERS AT MILE HIGH MINISTRIES

ISBN-13: 978-0-9852334-4-0

Library of Congress Cataloging-in-Publication Data is available upon request.

Design: Scot McDonald (www.chaireproductions.wordpress.com)
Cover art: iStock.com
Denver Street Saint illustrations by Brooks Hart

Photography: Katy Owens (www.facebook.com/katyowensphotography), Brien Hollowell (www.brienhollowell.com), Caleb Kohl (www.chlorofil.biz), Scot McDonald, Marisa Cole, and the Mile High Ministries staff.
Illustration: Scot McDonald

Printed in the United States of America
10 9 8 7 6 5 4 3 2

To our beloved city, Denver.

To the neighbors, volunteers, and supporters of Mile High Ministries with whom we have learned to seek God's peace for our city through the creative, compassionate, and prayerful development of people and communities.

"Blessed are the peacemakers, for they
will be called children of God."
— Jesus (Matthew 5:9)

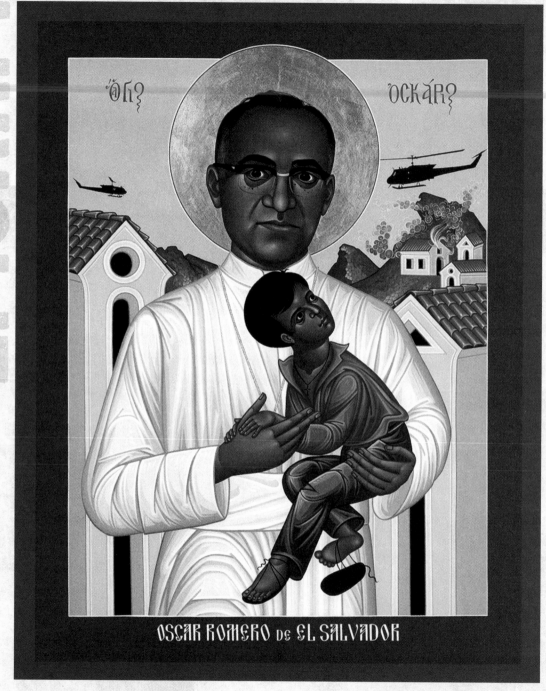

ΌΓΙΣ OCKÁRΣ

OSCAR ROMERO DE EL SALVADOR

Prayer of Óscar Romero

It helps, now and then, to step back and take a long view.
The kingdom is not only **beyond our efforts**, it is even beyond our vision.
We accomplish in our lifetime only a tiny fraction of the magnificent
enterprise that is God's work. Nothing we do is complete, which is a way of
saying that the Kingdom always lies beyond us.

No statement says all that could be said.
No prayer fully expresses our faith.
No confession brings perfection.
No pastoral visit brings wholeness.
No program accomplishes the Church's mission.
No set of goals and objectives includes everything.

This is what we are about.
We plant the seeds that one day will grow.
We water seeds already planted, knowing that they hold future promise.
We lay foundations that will need further development.
We provide yeast that produces far beyond our capabilities.

We cannot do everything, and there is a sense of liberation in realizing that.
This enables us to do something, and to do it very well.
It may be incomplete, but it is a beginning, a step along the way, an
opportunity for the Lord's grace to enter and do the rest.

We may never see the end results, but that is the difference between the master
builder and the worker.
We are workers, not master builders; ministers, not messiahs.
We are prophets of a future not our own.

—*by Bishop Ken Untener of Saginaw, composed in 1979 in honor of Archbishop Óscar
Romero of San Salvador.*

St. Oscar Romero was the Roman Catholic archbishop of El Salvador for three years, until his assassination in 1980. He was a passionate Christian voice for social justice, speaking out against violence and oppression. Romero was canonized as a saint by Pope Francis on October 14, 2018.

This prayerful reflection was actually written in Romero's honor by Fr. Ken Untener of Saginaw, Michigan as part of a sermon. It has become widely known as "The Prayer of Oscar Romero," and was used in a homily by Pope Francis in 2015. These words have encouraged the Mile High Ministries staff through the years, particularly at times when our work seemed small, incomplete, or even a complete failure.

TABLE OF CONTENTS

Opening to the Season
Prayer for the Season
Centering Scripture
Contemplative Practice
Peacemaking Practice
Perspectives
Urban Pilgrimage
Denver Street Saints
Denver Holy Days
Transformation
Public Action
Benediction
Wisdom

OUR STORY

RESOURCES

INTRODUCTION

The book you are holding is a creation of Mile High Ministries, written on the occasion of our thirtieth anniversary. It's a book *by* Mile High Ministries, but not exclusively *about* Mile High Ministries. It is a book about the city from which we take our name: Denver, the Mile High City. It's about particular ways of being and seeing that we have learned from our city over these thirty years.

As the title suggests, it is a book about *peacemaking*—the word we've chosen to describe our particular blend of community development and contemplative Christian spirituality. It also describes the legacy of "street saints" from Denver's history and countless people who today "seek shalom"– the holistic peace and prosperity of our city in ways that extend to all of our neighbors. "Blessed are the peacemakers," Jesus said, "for they shall be called children of God."

Mile High Ministries is both a non-profit organization and a spiritual community. We began in 1988 as a small group of mostly suburban churches who detected within the pages of scripture a heart for the poor. Over the decades we've become urban people, deeply connected to neighborhoods in the heart of our city. We put our ideals into action through community development efforts including supportive housing, legal services, job training, and leadership development. We have reclaimed and redeemed blighted places in Denver's urban core, creating small communities of compassion, hope, and healing.

As a spiritual community, the people of Mile High Ministries represent different streams of the Christian tradition who share a common commitment to the historic Christian faith and who share God's concern for the poor and marginalized. We help one another follow Jesus in lifestyles of generosity, peace, and self-emptying love. We pursue a contemplative path that helps us pay attention to how the Spirit is at work in our world.

We find joy in unleashing forces for good and recognize such goodness in the work of businesspeople, teachers, civic leaders and politicians, pastors, and countless neighbors who are quietly seeking the peace of our city at work or on their block.

We hope some of that abundant goodness comes through in the pages of our book, and that reading it helps you see and love your own city.

AS YOU READ...

Denver is a city of four distinct and meaningful seasons. *Beyond Our Efforts* is divided into four seasons—paying attention to the spiritual rhythms found in the seasons of the year, as well as to the longer seasons of our lives: seasons of new life and rebirth; seasons of passion and production; seasons of harvest and gratitude; and even seasons of waiting and death.

Each season of the book opens with poetry, prayer, and reflection on a passage of scripture. Next, we offer essays reflecting central aspects of the life and work we have been exploring during our thirty years of service in Denver:

- **Contemplative Practice** holds and centers us in the midst of busy programs and exposure to the trauma of our communities.

- **Peacemaking Practice** offers pictures of how we have come to understand asset-based community development.

- **Perspectives** on important words like help, hope, justice and generosity guide the pursuit of our mission: "We seek God's peace for our city through the creative, compassionate, and prayerful development of people and communities."

The next section of each season delves into our beloved city, Denver:

- **Pilgrimage** is an intentional spiritual journey, long or short, to a place that holds deep significance and perhaps even an opportunity to encounter the sacred. William Elliot puts it beautifully in his book *A Place at the Table* (page 157): "A pilgrimage is a moving meditation, a flow of reflective moments, a prayer rosary whose beads are places, and whose places point to one place—the heart."

- **Street Saints** are pioneering men and women, who are often unsung heroes whose presence within our "cloud of witnesses" inspires us to live an alternative story—pouring ourselves out on behalf of others.

- **Denver Holy Days** are seasonal events that capture the soul of our city. Any local magazine might highlight popular festivals, activities, and concerts. We decided to highlight lesser-known annual events that celebrate the hidden beauty of our technicolored city.

On the conviction that we live our way into new forms of thinking more than we think our way into changed lives, we next chronicle moments of **transformation** and **public action** that help us be more awake, alive, and connected to our communities.

Benedictions and blessings at the end of each season help us frame movement from season to season.

Woven throughout the book is a narrative essay in five parts titled Beyond Our Efforts.

Thank you for engaging the prayers and practices that have come to shape our life as a spiritual community and non-profit organization.

BEYOND OUR EFFORTS:
Contemplation

[
It helps, now and then, to step back and take a long view.
—Prayer of Oscar Romero
]

On a Tuesday morning in a warehouse district of Denver, I sit in silence. Eyes closed, feet on the floor, hands limp in my lap. In the quiet, my attention narrows. I feel the edge of the chair under my legs, the soft weight of my shirt on my shoulders, and the stir of breath across my lips. Inward, inward, I inhale. I am inside of my filling chest; ribs expand around me. Without effort, I pulse.

I am here now. I am nowhere. Nothing that mattered so much now matters.

The stillness holds.

I sit in this solitude with 20 of my friends. We are circled.

Around the circle we sit in our own silences, with our own breaths and pulse and flesh pressed into plastic chairs. Each with so much that is well with us and so much that is the matter with us. So many concerns, tasks, aches, and desires. So many sensations in body and spirit to catch the flow of breath, and thoughts to snag the busy brain.

Someone sighs.

In the center of our circle burns a flame.

Beyond the circle lies bathrooms, a kitchen sink piled with dishes that peeves our boss, and a conference room with its strategy-filled whiteboard. Outside the double doors sit restless people in the lobby, earlybirds for their appointments with our team, weighted with matters their lives depend on. Large north windows open upon a vista of a junkyard stacked with wrecked car frames, and above barbed wire rises our city's downtown skyline. South windows stream sunlight.

I scratch my nose, shift, and settle. "Beloved," I murmur, a word sacred to me. Air across my lips, inward. Air across my lips again, outward.

I accomplish nothing here, now. Nothing at all.

Together we are accomplishing nothing, this circle of 20 on the weekday clock.

Beyond the circle is Joshua Station, a motel home for dozens of formerly homeless girls, boys, moms, and dads who matter greatly to us. Like us, they wrestle addictions, hurt loved ones, mess up jobs, feed egos, and shame themselves. Like us, they work their plans, celebrate successes, heal wounds, and hug those most dear. We partner. The collaboration demands sophisticated expertise and savvy from my circle of friends; by comparison, running a regular motel must be a snap.

A quarter of a million cars rush past this motel each day on I-25. The highway serves as a major artery for Denver's daily urban system,

Beyond the circle is Joshua Station, a motel home for dozens of formerly homeless girls, boys, moms, and dads … Like us, they wrestle addictions, hurt loved ones, mess up jobs, feed egos, and shame themselves.

ebbing and flowing for five million people living along the Front Range. Beyond the freeway flows the South Platte, carrying snowmelt from the Continental Divide. Sometimes I walk under the overpass and along the river to Confluence Park in Lower Downtown, where William Russell's party searched for gold 160 years ago. The shallow river moseys, and ducks nose around its banks. Three hundred million years ago, according to most geological theories, plate tectonics pushed up the Rocky Mountain spine. The star that melts snow for our city and our dish-filled kitchen sink is 4.6 billion years young, and has maybe 5 billion good years left before it starts winding down. By that time the universe will reach a drinking age of 21 billion years, eager for a lifetime ahead. Maybe by that time there will be new theories about the universe—but it does help, now and then, to step back and take a long view.

Ha! Helps? In the long view, we are so very small.

Our lives are short, and our days shorter still. Our task lists are long. Almost a thousand of our Denver neighbors will sleep tonight under bridges, in cars, in parks, and in alleys—and another four thousand have no stable address. It's economic boom time for our boom-and-bust gold rush, cowpoke, oil shale, tech recreation town, and our most vulnerable neighbors can't hold jobs due to internal and external challenges we might help them address. It's a tenuous season for our social fabric, wedging good wills apart and pushing outsiders further outside. If only we had more staff and money and smarts! And a few dozen more hours in the day.

So we sit.

It's not so easy, sitting! I know, cue the eye rolls. But *you* try it—I dare you. No fair, doesn't count if you're not from a Western culture;

you have a head start and that's cheating. Fair game if you're driven. Driven to close more real estate deals, play bigger venues, increase membership, raise a healthy family, finish watching season four, or "develop people and communities" (to cite our own mission-driven organization).

Sit. Sit in our circle, accomplishing nothing, for there is so very much of utmost importance to accomplish. Place your feet on the floor, your hands in your lap, and your back straight against the chair. Close your eyes; breathe. Sit in silence. Sit with intention: intention only of releasing, knowing you are held, centered, and circled. If thoughts and sensations intrude, gently release them. This is prayer. Not the sort of prayer that entreats or exclaims or thanks or ceremonializes—all of which I do with sincerity, and much more easily. It is prayer of undoing, and to be undone is utterly transformational for all of us who are prone to more human doing than human being.

Pull up a chair, and if you are like us, your stillness will go well… for a matter of seconds, *tops*. Your mind or cell phone will buzz. Your nose will itch. A comment heard yesterday, or decades ago, will irk. Milk's running low; you'll add it to the list. Someone in the circle is attractive. A news clip from this morning disgusts you, the more you think about it. Someone in the circle is creaking a chair.

With us, around the circle, you reflexively summon energy to manage such things by long-practiced effort. Yes you're one of us, and we're one of you—you contemplative activist rascal, floundering in a prayer you will never master. We are enmeshed long before and far beyond our efforts to connect. We are vulnerable. We breathe together our air into moist tissue; we warm to the sunshine; we ebb and flow with our

Close your eyes; breathe. Sit in silence. Sit with intention: intention only of releasing, knowing you are held, centered, and circled.

city's freeways and social struggles; we pulse with the river and the stars beyond.

We are less than a single minute into our twenty minute contemplative prayer. Oh yes, that. I remember my sacred word, *beloved,* and inhale again.

—*Scott Dewey*

Winter

BEYOND OUR EFFORTS

CELEBRATING Winter

"It is the life of the crystal, the architect of the flake, the fire of the frost, the soul of the sunbeam. This crisp winter air is full of it."[1]
—John Burroughs

THE WOMB OF CREATION

T.S. Eliot once wrote, "The end is where we start from."[2] And so we begin this book with the season of winter. It may seem like an unusual place from which to begin, when we prefer to start with the spring and its alluring gift of new life. But for ancient Hebrews, early Christians, and other people who were much more connected to the cycles of the earth, the New Year began in the cold and the dark.

As the weather becomes colder and the nights longer in our part of the world, we intuitively slow down. The deep voice of nature beckons us to match her pace. Leaves have fallen; branches are broken. Within and beneath the ice, nature allows death to replenish the earth. Jesus clearly took his cue from nature's rhythm when he said, "Amen, Amen, I say to you, unless a grain of wheat falls into the earth and dies, it remains alone. But if it dies, it bears much fruit."[3]

Life is a process of dying and rising; of pruning to make space for new growth. It is how the earth is renewed. Without this part of life's movement, we would not grow or experience newness. Slowing down, listening, reflecting, acknowledging what must change is not easy work—but it is a necessary beginning for us all.

The gift of darkness can be unfamiliar in these days of artificial light whenever we want it—with the flip of a switch or a click of an app on a cell phone. And no wonder; we feel much more in control of things we can see. But darkness re-presents us with the reality that we cannot see everything, let alone control most events, people, and situations.

Darkness is the womb of creation. Learning to trust in the dark, we trust that God is moving in all the places that we cannot see or manage. The beginning of the year calls us toward greater depth of vision for God's providence in the hidden processes of life.

Welcome, winter. Welcome, God!

—*Scott Jenkins*

WINTER GIFTS

O Beloved Creator
whose Spirit lives deep within us all,
may the dark and dormant days of the winter season
move us to value this time of year
through your gifts of waiting and awareness.

Slowly and intentionally call us to reflect on our life's journey:
what it is that we need to release;
and that which we desire to engage.

As the winter brings a death-like quality with its cold and ice,
may a genuine gratitude for our unique lives
rise from our hearts.

O Beloved Creator
who loves us all deeply.
Amen.

—Scott Jenkins

Mark 5:1-20

"Night and day among the tombs and
on the mountains he was always howl-
ing and bruising himself with stones.
When he saw Jesus from a distance, he
ran and bowed down before him; and
he shouted at the top of his voice."
Mark 5:5-7

Restoring Fractured Humanity

When Ted launches into one of his angry outbursts in the middle of the sermon, it's hard to not be frightened, intimidated, or offended. On some Sundays in our little urban church, his explosive bipolar disorder makes it impossible for him to hold back. Enduring one of Ted's rages is a litmus test for our first-time visitors, and when his anger spills into the streets, our neighbors lock the doors and call the police.

I used to be scared of Ted myself. When we first met, he was homeless and smoking meth. I thought of him as I imagined the "demoniac" in chapter five of Mark's gospel. In that account, Jesus steps ashore in a region called the Gerasenes to a chaotic welcome from a bloodied, buck-naked, hysterical man. To his neighbors, this man was a menace. They banished him to the edge of town "among the tombs," in a graveyard that doubled as a massive pig farm.

Friendships with people such as Ted re-orient my reading lenses for such gospel stories. What would this demonized man be diagnosed with today, I wonder? What are the roots of his torment? Gerasenes was heavily occupied by the Roman military in units called "legions," I learn. I reflect on countless individuals I've met who have survived intense military combat in places like Afghanistan or Iraq, and now live on the streets with severe PTSD and drug addiction. I've heard in their voices the cries from among Gerasene tombs.

I once told Ted, "I pray you can one day feel the freedom to be completely yourself."

In response, Ted held his hand about three feet above the ground. "Ryan, I haven't felt the freedom to be myself since I was this tall. That's when the abuse, fighting, and rage started."

When society labels someone a menace, a nuisance, a criminal—or in this gospel story, a "demoniac"—it grants permission to perceive the person as less than human. At some point we all participate in the dehumanizing of another.

This is why the way of Jesus deserves special attention. Jesus ventures way off course to encounter this desperate man. Gerasenes was not his turf. More than that, Jews faithful to Levitical law did not converse with spirits or walk through graveyards—much less pig farms. Or was Jesus in fact exactly *on course*—for the work of restoring the horribly fractured humanity of a beloved one made in God's image?

In radical hospitality among the lonely, working for justice among the oppressed, and creating a culture of kinship on the margins of society, we begin by suspending assumptions and judgments. Prompted by holy curiosity, we're sure to discover there's always more to the story.

—*Ryan* Taylor

AN INNER SANCTUARY
Centering Prayer

At Mile High Ministries we meet daily for centering prayer. Typically there might be five of us, though sometimes we fill our little chapel with ten. Some days I sit and pray alone.

We are busy people. We choose to withdraw to this quiet place, away from clients and tasks, so that we can emerge restored, energized, and attentive to the needs of the hurting and poor among us—while more humbly mindful of the poverties we bear within ourselves.

The poor teach us much about self-emptying surrender to God. The families we serve have faced many losses—of possessions, relationships, and dignity. We join with them in a small act of spiritual solidarity, as we relinquish our illusions of control in this way of prayer. Each time we let go of what distracts us and return to God, we practice freedom from attachments and addictions so we can be fully present.

Winter leads us well in this form of prayer. The world becomes still, plants rest, and soil renews beneath the frosty surface.

During this season we hunker down with a small heater and a few blankets in the cozy chapel. The 20 minutes of community, sacred space, intimacy, and deep rest in God reorients each of us. Throughout the rest of my day, as things pull me out of a centered space, I gently speak my sacred word—reminded of the place within me connected to and longing for God, an inner sanctuary.

—*Amy Jackson*

GUIDELINES FOR CENTERING PRAYER

Choose a sacred word as the symbol of your intention to consent to God's presence and action within. This word is not a mantra to recite or a theme to focus on, but simply a reminder to return to stillness when you notice your thoughts wandering (and they will!). Examples of a sacred word might be: God, Love, Trust, Rest. Choose one word you'll stick with in your prayer times.

Setting a timer can help, so that you can let go of time and sink into God's loving embrace. Twenty minutes is typical, but you can adjust.

Sit comfortably and attentively. Many prefer eyes closed, feet flat on the floor, hands on lap. Settle your mind and body by noticing the gift of your breath, inhaling and exhaling life.

Silently introduce your sacred word as you enter into silence. As thoughts and sensations arise, allow them to arise and then fall away gently. If you notice your attention being carried with them, quietly say your sacred word as a reminder to release those thoughts and return to the center of silence.[1]

The Gift of Dignity

Wide open eyes

and hearts. Anticipation. Human worth. Poured-out love. Eagerness to give. Each year at our Christmas Store, I see these marvelous qualities expressed in the faces of shoppers and volunteers alike.

It just seems natural, and right, to give free toys to families struggling during the holidays. But we began to wonder if there was a more helpful way to help.

Years ago, Bob Lupton[1] helped us see contradictions in our Christmas giveaways: our theology of God's image in humanity suggests dignity and kinship, but our praxis told a different story. Paying closer attention to our families' demeanor during handouts and afterward, we noticed parents who were ashamed that outsiders supplied gifts for their children. Like all of us, they wanted to meet their own family's needs. Unable to provide, Dad often preferred to avoid holiday gatherings. Grandma managed a smile while her grandkids tore into gifts from strangers—glad for their excitement, but missing out on having chosen the perfect gift. If a sibling or friend was sponsored by a family that could afford more luxurious presents, there was yet another point of contention.

Together with our generous donors we had good intentions, but the mixed outcomes bothered us.

The Christmas Store is unique—instead of inviting families to endure a chaotic giveaway scene, we all share a holiday celebration where everyone contributes. Parents come to shop, without their children—much like you or I would. Aisles of new toys are donated and subsidized by generous community partners for parents to purchase at a steep discount. We all like a bargain, and seeing the smiles on the faces of the shoppers as they prepare for Christmas fills our hearts. Mom, dad, and grandparents get to shop for their family, knowing that Na'shai wants nail polish and Andrew needs a pair of headphones, and they don't have to guess whether a pre-wrapped donated gift will bring joy. This is an opportunity for low-income families to participate in the joy of giving, which includes saving, purchasing, and giving gifts themselves.

This is an opportunity for low-income families to participate in the joy of giving, which includes saving, purchasing, and giving gifts themselves.

The final station in the Christmas Store is a hospitality room offering hot cocoa and homemade cookies. Longtime shoppers and volunteers reconnect, catching up as carols play. I will always remember Katie's tears of joy; "Thank you so much for inviting me to come shop here, I was so worried this year knowing I couldn't afford rent, food, and gifts for my five kids."

Even more special, shoppers often volunteer! Dedicated workers and ministry partners mark their calendars every year for this special day. The Christmas Store is not a perfect system, and we continually tweak our approach. But in a season that can be overwhelming and heartbreaking for many, it reinforces dignity as we open our hearts for God's gifts of love.

—Rebecca Mendoza Nunziato

ANYTHING HELPS?

From Us and Them... to Kinship

**We choose to stand with the "disposable" so that the day will
come when we stop throwing people away.**
—Father Greg Boyle[1]

Something didn't sit right with me.

I felt that it was the right thing to do—an act of charity, full of
heart—but why was it so uncomfortable? I had fed the homeless
many times in my life, especially during the holidays: with my family
for the Salvation Army Thanksgiving Feast, during a prayer-fast in
downtown Denver, on a college service trip to the Seattle Rescue
Mission, offering hot cocoa on the 16th Street Mall with my church.

While serving, I heard many stories of love, addiction and loss
that touched my heart. Serving people in need was an essential part
of my journey of understanding people of other backgrounds. I also
came to see that food pantries and soup kitchens are vital anchors
in our city for emergency services. I am eternally grateful for these
opportunities that shaped me in my developmental years.

So why was I uneasy?

I had to admit I increasingly hated reaching over the counter to
serve a scoop of casserole to homeless men and women. I tried to
smile, make eye contact, and offer a sense of warmth—but it just
didn't seem to penetrate the barrier between "us" and "them." What
was the barrier? Was it the physical counter? Was it our vastly different worlds—visible in my freshly shampooed hair and new pair
of prescription glasses, across from their scruffy beards and sunken

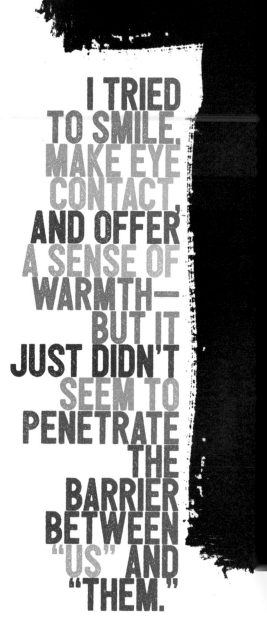

I TRIED TO SMILE, MAKE EYE CONTACT, AND OFFER A SENSE OF WARMTH—BUT IT JUST DIDN'T SEEM TO PENETRATE THE BARRIER BETWEEN "US" AND "THEM."

eyes? Was it the fact that daily, a new crew of energetic volunteers bustled in to scoop the food? Were they ashamed? Was I?

I'm glad for this moment because it pushed me to wrestle with my motives and assumptions. I remember as a child learning to distinguish between myself and others. Around the age of 11, kids on the playground would hold their arms up to mine and note the differences in our skin tones. We caught on to hair types and body shapes. Eventually, the distinctions included skills on the basketball court or in music class, house sizes, family vacations or brands of clothing. It is a natural way to begin to understand the world around us. But I came to see how these distinctions, while often rooted in innocent curiosity, can grow into vicious weeds of cruelty and discrimination.

I read what I could from academics and practitioners. Our "us and them" mentality lies deep in our subconscious, even if it runs counter to our more noble beliefs and values. Generations of humans have formed their tribes by determining who is "in" and who is "out." Experts call this *implicit bias*, because without intending, we cast our judgements on street corner panhandlers, feel suspicious of women in hijabs, or feel uneasy when we walk by a large African-American man.

We aren't bad people for having brains socialized to react this way; much of it is the result of a global history of racism and tribalism. Nor is this story new to 21st century America or us soup servers. It is the story of human (un)civilization, and for that reason it takes much compassion, awareness and spiritual sensitivity to understand how our biases, fears, and habits create barriers—and then begin to heal our unjust social arrangements.

Perhaps then, I wasn't crazy for feeling the distance between myself and the homeless, and for being troubled by the nagging presence of shame in the soup kitchen. We were replaying a familiar narrative with our ladles and empty bowls. Inheriting the sins of our forefathers and foremothers, even our most noble actions can leave us unable to see the full *imago dei* of those "in need." I longed to cross the divide, but I felt stuck.

If I am honest, *this recurring discomfort made me want to quit serving the homeless.*

In retrospect, I am glad it did.

With the help of longtime city leaders and wise sojourners among the poor, I quit a bad habit of "serving" the homeless. This habit, born in love and concern, was actually a subtle submission to a narrative I now refuse to believe: that there are those who are helpers and those who need help; those who "have" and those who "have not;" those who are in and those who are out—of society, God's family, or the like. I never verbalized these categorizations, but I came to see they were driving my charitable acts.

I didn't realize there was an alternative. Charity becomes toxic when the fuzzy feeling allows momentary gratification for the "givers" but creates little long-term change possibility for the "receivers." On "annual serve days" or at Christmas giveaways, kind-hearted volunteers flood in to give back to their community, while the poor file in to have their basic needs met—often averting their eyes, feeling grateful but embarrassed.

When offering charity in this way, I found my own sense of pride and worth unhealthily exalted while people on the receiving end felt their scarcity exposed. This imbalance is an example of *helping that hurts.*[2] I truly wished my giving

> I NOW REFUSE TO BELIEVE: THAT THERE ARE THOSE WHO ARE HELPERS AND THOSE WHO NEED HELP; THOSE WHO "HAVE" AND THOSE WHO "HAVE NOT;" THOSE WHO ARE IN AND THOSE WHO ARE OUT—OF SOCIETY, GOD'S FAMILY.

could be less impersonal and more aligned with God's vision of oneness among people.

Of course, the barriers I felt in the soup kitchen didn't melt away the moment I recognized these cerebral errors. It took spending time with people like Paul.

With sunken eyes and scruffy beard, chronically homeless and battling mental illness, Paul is a most enthusiastic and consistent church member. I met Paul when he asked to join our local outreach team—a group of volunteers devoted to befriending families in one of Denver's poorest neighborhoods. Ironic? Incredible.

Paul's participation and eventual friendship was one of the gateways for my transformation. Paul has his addictions, and I have mine. I was addicted to helping, and Paul helped me quit. Paul never asked for a dime, which still confounds me. He regularly finds treasures in the Denver alleyways and dumpsters and offers them as gifts. Paul helped me move past sympathy, past an analysis of his station in life as tragic, and into true kinship.

I'll never forget a day I felt disappointment and despair about our nation's politics. I wallowed on my couch thinking of friends who would be affected. Then I decided to call Paul. He didn't care to talk politics and instead told me stories of car racing and fishing. We laughed for twenty minutes straight.

Isn't that good news? I got out of my head, away from my ideological ideals, and I moved towards my friend. My wise, resilient, hilarious friend.

So, does *anything* help? I've learned that, no, not everything is helpful—for me or for my homeless friends. Our humanity is bound up with one another, and my toxic charity had found a way to deepen the divide of "us" and "them" rather than bridging and binding us together in love and kinship.

God continues to call us to care for the orphan, widow, foreigner, and poor because it is for our healing. Our global healing depends on an ongoing journey *toward* one another, which we may discover to be an experience of divine presence. You're invited—as we all are, and always have been—to the bountiful banquet table. Bring your beauty and bring your affliction, bring your serving spoon AND your empty bowl, and you'll find yourself in good company.

—*Rebecca Mendoza Nunziato*

RIVERSIDE CEMETERY

"TEACH US TO REALIZE THE BREVITY OF LIFE, SO THAT WE MAY GROW IN WISDOM."
—PSALM 90:10[1]

Behold a Severe Beauty

The gift of exploring the severe beauty of Denver's Riverside Cemetery is the invitation to face our own mortality. We invite you to spend some time at Riverside for a reflective, prayerful exploration of a landmark in the lives and deaths of our city.

The Birth of a Graveyard

Riverside was founded in 1876—the same year Sitting Bull defeated Custer at the Little Big Horn and the year Colorado became a state. On the inner bank of the South Platte, five miles northeast of downtown, Riverside was Denver's first alternative to "Boot Hill" (today's Cheesman Park). For decades, this memorial park was an irrigated oasis of forested green on an endless expanse of dry prairie.

Take in the View

The ground slopes away to the north, offering magnificent views of snow-covered Longs Peak— an expansive view, because there are virtually no trees. A combination of lost water rights and rising costs made it impossible to keep the park green in Colorado's high desert. Riverside had been slowly drying up for decades when the water was cut off in 2003. Most of the trees were already gone by then, especially after a beetle infestation in the 1960's. The few that are left today are dying of thirst—except, apparently, the noxious but tenacious "Trees of Heaven" whose suckers pop up around and through neglected graves.

The faintest breeze ruffles sparse patches of prairie grass. Natural grasses are watered only by Denver's occasional thundershower, which is enough for these hardy species to grow and to create a nearly impossible task for Raoul and Oscar. These two caretakers have maintained Riverside virtually by themselves for over three decades—a task made more difficult by a supply of one lone lawn mower.

A steady flame is held aloft just beyond the eastern boundary of the cemetery. Eternal flame honoring the dead? No—only the flare stack of an oil refinery. Although massive smokestacks from ore smelters were long ago demolished, Riverside continues to be encircled by the stacks of refineries and power plants. You are in the heart of Denver's industrial area. And yet, you may encounter white-tailed deer or a family of wild turkeys near the wetlands along the northeast edge of the cemetery.

Reflecting among Gravesites

Some impressive monuments remain, especially rising above Block 7—the circle drive at the center of the park where the scions of early Denver bought the first and best lots. One of the more prominent landmarks alerts us to the grave of... nobody: James Archer was instrumental in bringing both railroad and gas lighting to Denver, so it's no surprise to see his noble statue atop a tall pedestal. But nobody lies beneath. Oddly, he had the monument erected and the gravesite prepared

before his death, but elected to be buried back east.

One of Riverside's three mausoleums near Block 7 also lies empty. Hartsville Jones nearly became mayor once. After his first wife (forty years his junior) died, he remarried and then passed away not long thereafter. When yet a third woman showed up also claiming to have been his wife and the mother of his children, his burial in the mausoleum was thrown into chaos and was never finalized. Somehow such stories of emptiness seem congruent with this place.

Reflect: *Have you considered your intentions for your own body after death?*

Denver Heroes

Clara Brown was a Denver pioneer and successful entrepreneur and philanthropist. Her gravestone can be found just about at the midpoint of Block 25, looking to the east. (You can read about Clara on page 44.) *Read Clara Brown's story as you pause at her graveside—and pray for more such generous and resilient peacemakers for our city.*

Silas Soule was from an abolitionist family in Kansas and participated with his family in the underground railroad when he was only 15. In November of 1864, as an officer in the First Volunteer Cavalry Regiment, Soule refused to have the men

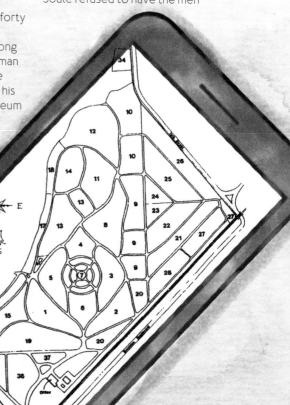

under his command fire upon Cheyenne and Arapaho people at Sand Creek, and later blew the whistle on atrocities that took place there. He was murdered months later, probably in retaliation. The Southern Arapaho honored Soule in 2014, 150 years after Sand Creek.

Reflect: *Consider the revolutionary acts of this brave Denverite and pray for courage for our generation in the face of injustice.*

Rich and Poor

Trains rumble along the southern edge of the cemetery, close to Silas's grave. The construction of these tracks during the silver-driven boom days of the 1880s brought the first hint of decline for Riverside: soon slaughterhouses appeared along the tracks, then ore-smelters with their massive smokestacks belching thick, black, poisonous smoke. When Fairmount Cemetery offered an alternative in 1890,

wealthy families removed the bodies of their loved-ones, making it more difficult for Riverside to pay its bills.

After wealthy families left, Riverside continued to welcome the bodies of the poor. The city of Denver bought small plots for $5 each in Block 12, burying the indigent or unidentified in unmarked graves. Even today, those who die with nothing and nobody are buried anonymously by the city in Block 33.

Reflect: *Take a moment to imagine one of our neighbors buried by city employees with no friends or family to mourn them. How might we make that situation a bit less likely?*

Behold a Severe Beauty

Our Centering Scripture for this season (page 30) took us to another graveyard, where Jesus encountered a man haunted by demons, isolated from his community. When I heard that story as a child in Sunday School, the only graveyard I knew how to imagine was one with manicured lawns, flags, and flowers placed lovingly on gravestones. Riverside helps me set the story in a more barren place. **Reflect:** *What perspective might a walk in this austere*

landscape, so near and yet so far from the cool and "relevant" places in our city, offer for connecting with the spiritual possibilities of seemingly desolate places?

Riverside Cemetery is beautiful. But it holds a severe beauty, with its collision between desolation and consolation in disorienting proximity. As you walk its dusty trails, consider Belden Lane's observation: "There is an unaccountable solace that fierce landscapes offer to the soul. They heal, as well as mirror, the brokenness we find within."[2]

Reflect: *What solace do you find in this place? What resources for your own healing? How is brokenness mirrored back to you?*

Over my years of wandering through Riverside, I have felt compelled to pay attention to the humble gravestones lining my path, details often obscured as soft sandstone melts away over the decades, yet each one telling a story. All the stories are sad in that they end the same way: death. I stumbled across a spot where twelve-year-old Jessie lies next to both of her rather young grandparents (or possibly her much older parents), each of whom had died not long after Jessie. I can only imagine that it might have been from their broken hearts, having lost their little loved one. We all live. We all die. All of us.

Teach us, God—even with the help of Riverside Cemetery—to realize the brevity of life, so that we may grow in wisdom.

—Jeff Johnsen

CLARA
BROWN

Clara Brown and Left Hand

Peacemakers in the Face of Discrimination and Tragedy

How does someone endure heartbreaking loss and yet persevere to live a life of generosity and self-emptying love?

Clara Brown was born into slavery in Virginia sometime around 1800. She married Richard when she was barely eighteen, and together they had four children. When Clara was thirty-five their owner died, and her family was separated—sold off to settle his estate. Clara was sold to a man in Kentucky, from whom she took her last name. For the next twenty years she raised George Brown's children instead of her own.

After earning her freedom at the age of fifty-six, Clara worked her way around the Midwest while searching for the family whom she had never stopped loving. In 1859 she landed a job as cook on a wagon train of gold-rushing miners heading west to the instant boomtown of Denver City.

First in Auraria and Denver, then in Central City, Clara worked as a laundress, cook, and midwife. She invested her earnings in mining properties and other real estate. Most gold-rushers met with disappointment and poverty. Clara managed to overcome persistent racial and gender discrimination to amass a modest fortune.

Yet by 1880, Clara was broke. She had been swindled numerous times by unscrupulous white businessmen. Several of her properties burned to the ground under mysterious circumstances. It was mostly her own generosity, though, that drained her fortune. In the words of the prophet Isaiah, she had spent herself "on behalf of the poor and needy."[1]

Clara had paid the way for at least sixteen former slaves to start new lives in Colorado and provided scholarships for young black women to study at Oberlin College in Ohio. She regularly took in sick and injured miners, nursing them to health at her own expense. Although she was Presbyterian, the first Catholic, Congregational, and Methodist churches in the Rocky Mountains were all built with generous donations from Clara Brown.

The prophet Isaiah promises that God hears the prayers of those who set the oppressed free and who share their food with the hungry. Yet near the end of her life Clara could not pay for her own housing and had to be taken in by a friend in Denver. Although she never stopped searching, it appeared that she would die without finding her lost family.

Then in February of 1882 Clara received news that one of her daughters, Eliza Jane Brewer, had been located! Clara didn't have money for a train ticket, so an anonymous donor paid for her to travel to Council Bluffs, Iowa to reunite with her daughter and granddaughter after forty-seven years of separation.

Clara Brown died in Denver on October 23,

1885. Her funeral was attended by mayors, governors, and other Colorado dignitaries. Clara's grave can be found near the east edge of Riverside Cemetery, not far from today's York Street.

WHEN ASKED WHERE SHE DREW THE STRENGTH TO LIVE AS SHE DID, CLARA BROWN SAID: "I JUST DO WHAT JESUS TELLS ME TO DO."

When asked where she drew the strength to live as she did—building a successful business in the face of relentless bigotry, spending herself on behalf of the hungry and satisfying the needs of the oppressed (Isaiah 58:10), all the while searching for loved ones from whom she had been separated by slavery's cruel disregard for the bonds of human family—Clara Brown said: "I just do what Jesus tells me to do."

When the wagon train led by Benjamin Wadsworth pulled up to the "Elephant Corral" (today's 14th and Wazee Streets) in the spring of 1859, its cook—Clara Brown—may have become the first African-American woman to reach the Pikes Peak region. She would have

NIWOT
(LEFT HAND)

seen the original inhabitants of the area—Southern Arapaho, led by Little Raven, as she passed their village on a low rise just a few yards away.

Another small Arapaho band in the area was led by Niwot, whose name translates to "Left Hand" in English.[2] Although the gold rush had only just begun, Niwot and his family had already watched thousands of white people travel through the region, including homesteaders on the Oregon Trail and Mormons sojourning to Utah.

Foreseeing that these strangers would bring to an end their lifestyle based on the buffalo, Left Hand and his wife embarked on a remarkable expedition. Traveling by horseback with their children, they journeyed through Nebraska and Iowa to learn about the life of the very people whose presence threatened their own livelihood and culture—to investigate how the Arapaho might pivot to become farmers and ranchers.

In April of 1860, Niwot's band was camped on high ground west of Denver, probably near today's intersection of Federal Boulevard and Colfax Avenue. While Niwot and most of the men were away on a hunt, a gang of drunken miners led by a man known as "Big Phil the Cannibal" rampaged through the village, raping many of the Arapaho women, including Niwot's sister—and perhaps also his wife and young daughter. Sensing that vengeance would stoke an endless cycle of violence, and accepting the assurances of white friends, Niwot prevailed upon his people to trust the white men's justice system. To their dismay, authorities in Denver did nothing about "Big Phil's" gang.

Over the next few years, Niwot tried desperately to hold his people together in the face of disease, starvation, and despair. His commitment to adapt to the overwhelming white presence rather than resist with violence cost him the respect of many of his own people.

As the saying goes, "what we see is behind our eyes." Behind many eyes, including those of Denver civic leaders, was the assumption that genocide was the only solution for the "Indian problem." After spending time with the Cheyenne, however, Denver founding father Major Edward Wynkoop made the shocking (to him) discovery that they carried a nobility and goodness rarely observed within his own community. (His advocacy for tribal peoples made him a social outcast later in life.) In September, 1864, Wynkoop brought a delegation of Arapaho and Cheyenne "peace chiefs" to meet with Governor Evans at Camp Weld (very near where Joshua Station stands today). Apparently behind the governor's eyes—and those of his military commander, John Chivington—were fear and fixed ideology. They refused to see the moment as pregnant with the possibility of peace.

Two months after the Camp Weld Council, Chivington would lead an army to the surprise slaughter of hundreds of unsuspecting Cheyenne and Arapaho—including children, women and older men—in their winter camp on Sand Creek. Of sixty Arapaho residents of the camp, four survived. Mortally wounded, Niwot struggled across frozen ground to a Cheyenne camp, dying a few days later.

Ignorance and fear of "the other" drove Evans and Chivington to violence. Niwot, capable of more nuanced thinking about the changing dynamics of his

HE AND CHEYENNE CHIEF BLACK KETTLE ONCE PAID AN EXPENSIVE RANSOM IN PONIES AND BUFFALO ROBES TO HOSTILE SIOUX AND CHEYENNE, AND EVEN OFFERED HIS OWN LIFE IN RANSOM TO BUY THE FREEDOM OF SEVENTEEN-YEAR-OLD LAURA ROPER AND THREE OTHER WHITE CHILDREN.

times, sought to understand his enemies and actively extended his hand in peace. He and Cheyenne Chief Black Kettle once paid an expensive ransom in ponies and buffalo robes to hostile Sioux and Cheyenne, and even offered his own life in ransom to buy the freedom of seventeen-year-old Laura Roper and three other white children.

"Blessed are the peacemakers," Jesus said, "for they shall be called the children of God."

In the spirit of Christ, we offer this blessing in honor of two children of God who lived in this place before us:

Blessed are you, Clara Brown of Denver and Left Hand of the Southern Arapaho, peacemakers and children of God. In the face of our own fear, division, and violence, may we learn to see as you saw and live as you lived. Amen.

—Jeff Johnsen

March

DENVER MARCH POWWOW

Healing Rhythms

Mother Earth's heartbeat reverberates through the Denver Coliseum every March. She announces herself in the banging of drums, the nimble footwork, the clanging of beads and bells, and the strong voices of Native American people. For over forty years, winter has melted into spring accompanied by the music of Powwow.

During our thirty years in Denver, we have grown to recognize the sacred importance of *place*. Places are endowed with significance through both beauty and affliction, and remembered through stories. The spaces we occupy and the very ground we stand upon are filled with profoundly beautiful stories—in which life was ushered in, hearts were wed, and friendships were born. Other stories are deeply painful—experiences of separation, death, suffering, or wrongdoing.

Denver's soul has been formed by the various peoples who have called the Front Range their own. Before this land was home to gold miners, ranchers, and tech entrepreneurs, it was home to the Arapaho, Cheyenne, and Ute tribes. Today, generations after the massacres of thousands of native people, the unjust treaties, the seizure of land, and the loss of liberty, Denver's indigenous peoples still gather to the healing sound of the drum.

At Powwow, the dance of beauty and affliction magnifies the sacredness of place. At this intertribal gathering the swirl of feathers, the fragrance of fry bread, the vividly patterned traditional clothing, and the ancient songs weave together a common thread of humanity. Each unique tribe and each individual dancer moves independently—but all to the heartbeat of one drum.

—*Rebecca Mendoza Nunziato*

49

DEATH AND HOPE AT JOSHUA STATION
A Story of Courage

"Hope does not disappoint." —Romans 5:5

We've all played the mental game, wondering, "what if I only had a few weeks left to live?" What would you do if you had a chance to prepare? For one such woman, Hilda Cortez-Chavez, the answer was clear: show up, be courageous, love greatly, and fight for her life until she could secure a safe and loving home for her young sons. This is exactly what she did, while knowing it was the beginning of saying "good-bye" at the age of 29.

When I met Hilda, she was engaged in a battle for her life. She found Mile High Ministries, became a client of the Justice and Mercy Legal Aid Center, and moved into the supportive housing community at Joshua Station. Hilda would be the first to tell you these programs saved not only her own life for a time, but the future lives of her two young sons. "This has been the best year of my life," she told us, of her final chapter on earth spent with us. From the outside looking in, this story is tragic and unfair: a young mother's experience filled with pain, suffering, injustice, and sadness. Yet in Hilda's story we find a miraculous story of redemption, love, vulnerability, and courage.

"This has been the best year of my life," she told us, of her final chapter on earth spent with us.

A passionate and fiery Mexican woman, Hilda did not shy away from speaking her mind and telling her truth. As *mama oso* ("mama bear") as they come, it was difficult for her to face the reality that her life was slipping away—knowing the impact of her struggle on her children. Her oldest son, only 12 years old, had the ambulance on speed-dial, ready to call every time she needed to be rushed to emergency dialysis. Her nine-year-old son was traumatized because of her diagnosis. Hilda hoped there was another way for her sons to experience life, both hers and theirs, but she was uncertain of the way forward.

When one potential adoptive family fell through, Hilda's hope began to fade. The disappointment was one more bitter twist amid a long journey of so many hardships and blows. Despair is commonly defined as "the absence of hope," but we saw in Hilda that hope and despair cannot be divorced from the other when it comes to confrontation with death. In this hard winter season of her life, they were uniquely woven together. Some imagine that becoming prepared for death in some way softens the blow. But for Hilda, the losses were not only present but future. For her sons soon to be left behind, every coming milestone, every failure, every moment of celebration would be marked by loss. She would not be there to offer them her embrace.

Yet "hope does not disappoint." It was a truth Hilda clung to, and showed us, in the darkness. We do grow restless, forgetting that rest and hope can be found among the stillness of winter. Spring does in fact come to bring new life. We were able to experience that together with Hilda.

With help from the Mile High Ministries community and a local adoption agency, the breakthrough Hilda sought for so long finally came. A loving couple stepped forward, ready to embark on the journey of parenthood. Hilda was blessed to spend several months getting to know this family and watching them with her boys, before returning to her home country to spend her final days with her father.

The timing of her death, which I fully believe was an intentional understanding between her and God, could not have been more beautiful or miraculous. In Mexico, Día de la Madre (Mother's Day) is May 10. It was

Due to Hilda's hope, courage, and sacrificial love, Hilda's sons were given new life.

as though Hilda deliberately fought to stay on this earth for her boys, whom she loved more than her own life, for one last Día de la Madre. The next day, Hilda breathed her last breath and surrendered her maternal rights to the woman she had hand-picked to nurture her boys for the rest of their lives. Mother's Day in the United States happened to fall on May 11, 2014, the same day of Hilda's passing.

Due to Hilda's hope, courage, and sacrificial love, Hilda's sons were given new life. Her story continues to live on through them. Through an extraordinary season of struggle and beauty, together with Hilda we lived to see for ourselves that "hope does not disappoint."

—*Dulce Garcia*

A LITURGY OF SACRED SIGHT
After Violence, Reclaiming Peace

Wednesday morning. Rush hour. Our little group huddles in the entrance to a downtown parking garage just steps away from the 16th Street Mall, one of Denver's most popular attractions. Layered with parkas and hoodies, bunched against a freezing wind, each of us struggles to hold a printed liturgy in our mittened hands. We wipe away snow that dusts the words as the first reader prays aloud:

Grace and peace to all of us in the name of our Loving God. This space that was traumatized by senseless violence, we reclaim as a place of life, community, and hope.

A few days earlier on the very spot where we stood, a random argument between two strangers escalated, ending in a gunshot. A father of two small children lay dead.

We ask that God may grant us peace. That in our pain we may find comfort, in our confusion we may find a measure of understanding, in our sorrow we may find hope, and in the aftermath of fear we may find strength and healing.

We are an informal network of friends[1] who gather when someone dies violently near one of our homes, churches, workplaces, or other places we share life connection. We call it a Liturgy of Sacred Sight: by faith we practice *seeing life* in places haunted by death—even if we have to squint. By determined faith, we dare to speak of God's presence in seemingly godforsaken corners of our city. We've touched our fingers to the blood-spattered walls of a stoop where two young friends once sat and talked, unaware that death was stalking them.

We confess that this tragedy is part of a wider failure of community. We long for communities where everyone can belong, feel safe, and experience the simple dignity of respect for their life as a fellow human being.

We've met to honor the life of the newly dead in an alley between two warehouses in RiNo where a homeless man was killed for reasons unknown. Though our liturgy has space to speak the victim's name, we can only stumble into a sacred pause here—as his name is likewise unknown to authorities.

Our brother _____, we see you. We acknowledge your death and your life. You did not leave this world unnoticed. We hold your memory in our love and care. We affirm that your life was and is treasured by God.

By the lovely pavilion at City Park we mourned the shooting of a police officer. In the face of such appalling violence we choose to hold the gaze of the victim, and much more challenging, of the perpetrators. To recognize their common humanity, amid so much that has been ruptured.

We welcome all persons, all conditions, and all emotions to this gathering—as we trust the process of love and healing within and around us.

No sound but wind rattling dry grass as we stand in a vacant field along train tracks on the north edge of Swansea. A group of addicts meet here to shoot up on a discarded couch under a cottonwood tree. A young

woman the same age as one of our daughters—and with the same name—was stabbed to death here. Her body stuffed into a nearby dumpster. Our words feel inadequate as we invite healing from God's Spirit.

Be still and know that I am God.
Be.

We've gathered multiple times on one particular corner on the East Side, where many young people have lost their lives outside a busy convenience store. Lined up against the curb of a noisy street, we shout solemn prayers over the din.

May the resurrection be experienced in Denver today, as enemies are moved toward reconciliation, exclusion becomes embrace, and as voices of criticism and hate are transformed into encouragement. God, we ask your blessing on this neighborhood.

We pluck a plant growing through cracks in the asphalt and use it to sprinkle water on the place and on those who are gathered.

As we sprinkle this water, we recognize you, Holy Spirit, in this place. Redeem this space and community from the pain and loss that occurred here. This place that has been subjected to fear, anger, and pain, we reclaim for the world as a place of hope and community.

One May morning in our neighborhood, we stood on a freshly blood-stained sidewalk for the first of what would be two liturgies that day. Two murders, connected with one another. Before us in the weeds was a makeshift memorial with teddy bears, candles, and love notes. A young father had been gunned down as he was leaving the funeral of his uncle, who himself had been murdered days earlier.

Our group was larger than normal and included a Black Lives Matter local leader, a philanthropist with right-wing politics, an evangelical preacher from the suburbs, an entrepreneur, and some young neighborhood leaders. Just then, a passing car slowed and came to a stop before us. We were a bit on edge after the recent events, and wondered if this meant trouble. Out of the car and into our circle stepped a trembling woman. "I'm his mother," she said of the man whose death had brought us there.

We asked if she wished to pray with us. She said no, but then leaned in to join us as we continued the "litany of deliverance" portion of the ceremony:

From the brutality of murder and violence
Save us, O God
And from all evil,
Save us, O God

This grieving mother served notice, if we needed it, that this holy ground was not ours. She expressed no resentment; only anguish. And how the anguish gushed! This place of violence was terrible strange ground for her even more than for us.

Blessed are those who mourn.
For they will be comforted.

As our liturgy concluded, we simply held one another. The grieving mother finally broke the silence by asking for help with counseling services she couldn't afford. Heads, hearts, and hands came together to offer support from our wildly diverse cohort.

We don't make a big deal of these ceremonies. We don't call the media or make any effort to attract crowds. We let neighbors know, when we can. People passing by are often curious, and we invite them into our circle.

Do we really think that we can stem the tide of violence—not to mention the deeper crisis of hope from which it springs—or that we can "reclaim" a place of death with our awkward little prayers? We are people of faith, but we're also realistic about the ongoing work to be done, and pledge to do what we can:

We commit ourselves to building community that is humane, compassionate, just, and filled with dignity.

Our Liturgy of Sacred Sight group is small; our prayers, just words on a page. By faith, however, we hold each of these moments sacred as we lean into the communion of the living and the dead, together with the One who has tasted death and resurrection.

Our little group glances around one last time at what would have been the final sights of our dying neighbor. We receive this benediction, which we also share with you:

May we go forth in the name of the Father who is for us, the Son who is with us, and the Spirit who unites us all in the never-ending dance of love. Amen.

—Jeff Johnsen and Scott Dewey

Be still and know
that I am God.
—Psalm 46:10

Our weekly staff gatherings often begin with a centering practice called the "Be Still Prayer." Usually I find it easier to silently wait for the voice of God when I am alone. In a group I can be distracted with things waiting for us all to attend to—"our real work." Recognizing that challenge, we share this practice together because it helps us be more fully present and attentive to God.

Be Still Prayer

Philip Yancey suggests a progression of the two commands of Psalm 46:10; the first prepares us for the second.[1] "Be still," from the Hebrew verb *raphe*, means *to let go; to surrender.* "Know that I am God" involves not simply cognitive recognition, but becoming wholly centered in the power, love, and mercy of the Divine. Our simple way of praying this psalm involves subtracting words—a relinquishment that nudges us further into silence. Such prayer draws us deeper from conceptual thinking to simply being.

In this Winter season, may you find rest and peace in this simple prayer. Sit quietly and take a few deep breaths as you bring your presence to God. Speak or sing the Psalm in five consecutively diminishing sentences. You may wish to continue by reversing this order and repeating several times. Finish in silence, held by the love of God.

Be still and know that I am God.
Be still and know that I am.
Be still and know.
Be still.
Be.

—Penny Salazar-Phillips

I just do what Jesus

tells me to do.

—Clara Brown, Denver pioneer

BEYOND OUR EFFORTS:
Abundance

[*We water seeds already planted, knowing that they hold future promise.*
—Prayer of Oscar Romero]

We practice our ways of seeing.

A man on the phone tells me flatly, "That neighborhood is full of animals." I'm caught off guard with no reference point for his comment. I like animals. I like my neighborhood. I'm simply calling to inquire about a house for sale a couple blocks away from mine. "You don't want to buy it." My bewilderment deepens; he's listed as the seller.

In front of me, in line at the Denver airport, a man kneels to speak at eye level with a young boy. "Listen to me carefully son—this is important. Look around you. See all the people with different kinds of uniforms? People behind counters. People telling us where to go. People with badges. Never, ever forget: they are vermin. Do you know what vermin means? Every single one of them is trying to screw us. They will, if we let them. Are we going to let them?" Wide eyed, the boy shakes his head.

How we see matters, so we practice. We tend the soil of our souls, cultivating the direction toward which our tendrils stretch and our growth inclines. Of course other gardeners jostle among us with their own notions. There are external conditions; seasons and weather may be fair or harsh.

We practice.

"I fell in love with beauty there," a friend tells me of a dark time living in a meth house while addicted and removed from her children. "I took long walks every day, looking at nature. That's really what I remember most."

"I cannot breathe sometimes," confides a neighbor whose second son was gunned down on the street 10 years after her first. "And then a breath comes. And another. To be honest at first I didn't want to breathe. Still don't, some nights. Before all this, I never paid any mind to breathing. Like it or not, every one of those breaths is a gift of life. I see it now. I wake up and tell myself, just keep on breathing."

We practice.

> *I see the Lord*
> *Seated on the throne, exalted*
> *And the train of his robe*
> *Fills the temple with glory!*

The Anchor of Hope gospel choir soars with the prophet Isaiah's vision. Our hands rise, palms up, and our voices join the song:

> *And the whole earth is filled*
> *The whole earth is filled*

How we see matters, so we practice. We tend the soil of our souls, cultivating the direction toward which our tendrils stretch and our growth inclines.

The whole earth is filled
With his glory.

People leap to their feet, singing "Holy, holy, holy!" The crescendo stirs bodies and souls, sending us upward, then hovering with another stanza, and upward still. Even a black gospel anthem eases in for a landing eventually, however, so we sing again more softly: "The whole earth, the whole earth, the whole earth" a dozen times, two dozen times, until my brain intrudes with a very reasonable inquiry, asking, "The whole earth?" The *whole* earth?

My neighbor sways in her purple choir robe, drawing breath for each line of praise. Oh my dear church sister, whose two sons' blood drained onto asphalt on the very same Denver boulevard ten years apart, the whole earth? Glory?

We are practicing. It's an almost impossible stretch to believe what we are singing, but we keep drawing our breaths for another stanza. In contrast, a man is raising his young son in the nurture and admonition of reality as he sees it from the airport line: the whole earth is filled with malevolence. In every nook and corner lurks a threat. We must be vigilant. We must brace and defend.

Taken as a whole, presumably, our observable data points do not fundamentally differ. We live in the same city, the same world, tending our similarly human lives. True, privilege and trouble are maldistributed, which we might suppose nurtures more anxiety in the downtrodden.

But I discover that the real estate owner on the other end of the phone holds Colorado statehouse office. He has enriched himself as a slumlord by perpetuating his fearful stereotypes. Fines for city code violations are his only material threat, to which he responds with lawsuits. He pretends to be a victim forced into listing his blighted properties on the market, without ever actually selling. Many in the rousing church choir have lived in those rentals for decades, taking hold of their good and beautiful lives a breath at a time. They sing of what they see, flowing from how they see—the glory of the Lord and the earth, whole.

We "contemplative activists" practice a way of faith-filled seeing among such neighbors, listening and learning. Together with those who have breathed their breath of life into every forgotten corner and public plaza of our city, we cultivate abundance.

Learning to see, we commit to best practices in community development. We good-willed helpers unlearn and relearn how to see our own help. In dialogue with cutting-edge practitioners around the world, we find that the most effective responses to human need are not essentially responses to need at all. Deficit-oriented approaches flounder; asset-based initiatives unleash abundance. And the most dynamic and generative sources of abundance come not from outside the context of need, but from within!

This revolution for human flourishing finds expression under a variety of names and approaches: Asset-Based Community Development (ABCD), Appreciative Inquiry (AI), Participatory Learning, Asset Mapping, Community Organizing, Microenterprise Development, and Positive Psychology—to mention only a few disciplines worthy of our highest investment of theoretical study and practical application. It's a golden age of toolmaking for social change and empowerment.

Such tools require sight. Some people have wide eyes for abundance intuitively; others of us come resisting, struggling, and squinting. We

Learning to see, we commit to best practices in community development. We good-willed helpers unlearn and relearn how to see our own help.

exercise our eyes by practicing gratitude—for instance in the classical personal reflection of Examen, or in a thank-you note. We step out and walk, as my friend did daily from her meth house, and awaken to the natural world along our city sidewalks. A bitter experience crushes us, and then in time we breathe, breathe, breathe into a life that eventually surprises us with how it gleams. We grow to see—and sustain a way of seeing by refusing to break faith with goodness glimpsed.

It is very possible to stay small of sight, entrenched and defended, as my wary airport companions attest. With deficit-confined vision we must play it safe at best, or perhaps win at others' cost like our local neighborhood slumlord.

With abundance-liberated vision, however, we can risk. We can risk rest, in the face of pressing need. We can risk an audacious plan, with our credibility at stake, amid fears it might be our only shot. We can risk great sorrow, trusting we'll be held. We can risk our delight, trusting its own worthiness, and the worthiness of the world to share in it. We can risk a painful path of healing from whatever has us in its grip. We can risk a hard conversation, or a joke that might work if the timing's right. We can risk a song.

We practice. My, do we need practice! We nurture such vision tenderly, playfully, and fiercely in the world. With growing trust in what we've seen—and what we haven't yet beheld—we water seeds.

—*Scott Dewey*

Spring

BEYOND OUR EFFORTS

CELEBRATING Spring

Behold, the emerging
Spring
The fullness of hope held in the winter.

A time of awakening.
Whispering
A coming message—color and beauty.

Even now at our feet dead seeds of winter
Raise their heads bearing treasure.

O time of year that calls deserts to bloom,
Singing of birds is come like abundant rain.

Viriditas, the Greening

We are watching winter turn to spring in our city. Friends are walking the paths of the Botanical Gardens, filling their hearts with the blooming flowers and sharing rich conversation. Bird lovers scan the skies for pelicans, flickers, and red-wing blackbirds. Denver awakens to the song of the sparrow and robin. Japanese Plum trees along Speer Boulevard burst into vivid shades of purples, pinks, and whites.

St. Hildegard of Bingen (1098–1179 A.D.) was an artist, musician, scientist, and theologian who recognized a readiness in plants to receive the sun and to transform it into energy and life. To describe this, she often used the word *viriditas*, "the greening of things from within."

Spring is a generative time of renewal, rebirth, and a loving revival of life. We experience "the greening from within" not only in nature, but physically and spiritually from within ourselves as well. The poet Ronald Meseck says, "We are all planted, from that darkness life begins / from the seed that was sowed we commence to grow."

In my neighborhood near Sloan's Lake, gardeners are working the soil and planting. At Joshua Station, families are making lists of the things they want to plant in our community garden. Volunteers help till the soil.

Communities all around Denver are anticipating farmers' markets–Mo' Betta Greens adds a Five Points twist with DJ music serenading the harvest of tomatoes, squash, and strawberries.

As you plan your garden—even a porch or window plant!—think about non-profits in our city that work with the homeless, those in poverty, and those who live in food deserts (neighborhoods without accessible grocery stores). The GrowHaus is a nonprofit indoor farm in northeast Denver dedicated to food production, food education, and food distribution—plant sales are a great way for you to partner with them in spring. On the west side of town, EarthLinks cultivates transformation and self-worth with people experiencing chronic homelessness and poverty. It's a wonderful place to buy gifts or to volunteer.

Denver hosts many spring activities where you can join family and friends to celebrate. Mark your calendar to make merry at the Cinco de Mayo Festival, the Five Points Jazz Festival, the Colfax Marathon, the Denver Arts Festival, or the Denver Day of Rock.

The springtime of our lives stirs renewed spiritual thirst and awareness of God's movement. Through this season's celebrations of Passover and Easter, we remember Jesus' promise to make everything new.

"Viriditas" is a wonderful word of Spring. As you dance through our city and your life, can you embrace the greening? How will you engage Springtide in our city?

—*Penny Salazar-Phillips*

May the Rising Sun

O Creator God, maker of all that is, who always has been,
may the rising sun remind us of you and all you have created.
In this season of budding beauty, new birth and the gift of
   renewal are beheld.
Where deep calls to deep, give us eyes to see the bounty you
   call forth,
from the ground of the earth and from our souls.

Remind Us

May the meditations of our hearts become the Light.[a]
Crown us, O God with steadfast love.[b]
Anoint our heads with the overflowing cup of oil.[c]
Endow us with your great wisdom and strength.[d]

Beloved, we come overflowing. We thank you.
Our gratitude abounds and speaks of your goodness.

—Penny Salazar-Phillips

Scripture inspiration:
[a]Psalm 19, [b]Psalm 103,
[c]Psalm 23, [d]Psalm 37

Cultural inspiration:
"Prayer of the Four
Directions,"[1] from
various Native American
traditions, with East
representing dawn, light,
wisdom, and spring.

A Vibrant City

Be glad and rejoice forever
in what I am creating;
for I am about to create Jerusalem as a joy,
and its people as a delight.
I will rejoice in Jerusalem,
and delight in my people;
no more shall the sound of weeping be heard in it,
or the cry of distress....
Like the days of a tree shall the days of my people be,
and my chosen shall long enjoy the work of their hands.
They shall not labor in vain,
or bear children for calamity;
for they shall be offspring blessed by the LORD—
and their descendants as well.
Before they call I will answer,
while they are yet speaking I will hear.
The wolf and the lamb shall feed together,
the lion shall eat straw like the ox;
but the serpent—its food shall be dust!
They shall not hurt or destroy
on all my holy mountain,
says the LORD.

(Isaiah 65:18-19, 22-25)

Isaiah 65

The ancient Hebrew prophet Isaiah prompted imagination for a vibrant, healthy city where neighbors celebrate in the streets. And they have great reason for celebration! Here infant mortality is obsolete, lives are long, and meaningful work allows those who were once poor to prosper—living in homes they've built and eating the produce of their own gardens. There is a healthy mix of self-reliance with communal love and support.

Natural rivals—even enemies—dwell together in peace instead of violence.

Thousands of years later, how might the prophet's vision stir our own imaginations for what Denver can be, and how we might contribute?

In this prophetic depiction, God promises to listen when the city's people pray. As people of faith, we often pray for personal concerns or to cultivate our inner life—but how might we also pray for our city? In light of Isaiah's very practical urban vision, what might we express to God about our city's systems, economy, and built environments: streets and sidewalks, sewers and schools, healthcare and housing, policing and public transportation?

—Jeff Johnsen

LECTIO DIVINA

We city people hurry. We eat fast. We hustle out to wait in traffic. We flick around our phones—skimming, analyzing, and processing more information than humans have ever had handy. These fast-paced skills take us far, but not far enough. The greatest distance we can travel, as the saying goes, is the few inches from the head to the heart—contemplative activists venture on this journey, slowly.

Lectio Divina is an ancient practice of prayerfully savoring a sacred text, receiving it deeply into ourselves. "Lectio" means to read, and "Divina" suggests opening ourselves to the divine. We need practical help to be present, lingering with the words as we might with a fine meal. Monday and Friday mornings at Mile High Ministries we set aside twenty minutes to share Lectio as a group. Lectio typically consists of four movements, which in Latin lingo are *Lectio* (read), *Meditatio* (meditate), *Oratio* (speak), and *Contemplatio* (contemplate).

■ "Lectio" pronunciation: Latin geeks, including some old-school Catholics in our circles, tend to say "lexio." The rest of us pronounce it like it looks.

■ When doing Lectio together as a group, choose readers ahead of time for each movement. Invite sharing at the end of the second movement (inviting participants to speak their chosen words or phrases without comment), and the third movement (brief reflections on what they are hearing and experiencing).

■ Just a few verses is better for Lectio than a long passage. At Mile High Ministries we usually select the current week's gospel reading from the lectionary, which is a weekly scripture reading plan, set up in a three-year cycle, used by a great many churches of diverse denominations around the world. The Revised Common Lectionary can be accessed at www.lectionary.library. vanderbilt.edu—an excellent website for this scripture resource.

■ Oral reading is the way most people experienced scripture before the modern era of print and digital publication. Speaking and listening involves us on the level of physical sensation, engaging our whole selves more fully.

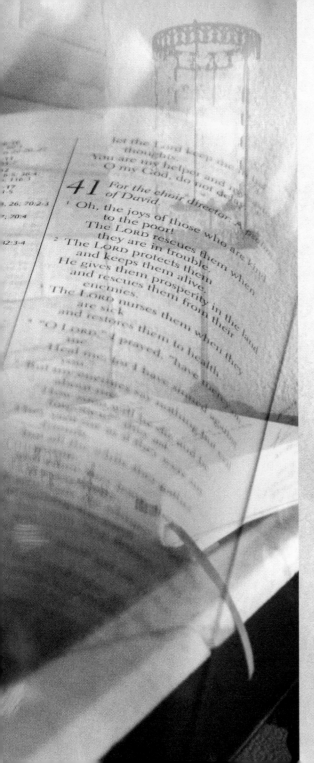

SAVORING THE WORD

To get started with Lectio, choose a few verses of scripture; perhaps a story from the Gospels or a portion of the Psalms. Get in a comfortable, attentive position and center yourself with quiet, simple breathing. When you are ready, move through the four phases of interaction—each time reading the passage aloud, following the prompts, and allowing spaces for quiet.

First Reading—Lectio: What does the text say?

Listen to the overall sense of the passage. Savor the words. Let your imagination enter the world of the text, open your heart and allow yourself to feel.

Second Reading—Meditatio: What is here for me today?

Does a particular word or phrase glimmer? Slowly repeat it, allowing it to interact with your inner world of concerns, joys, hopes, and memories. Is there an invitation here?

Third Reading—Oratio: How am I responding?

Speak to God in response, trusting that whatever you have to say is welcomed. Offer to God what you experienced today by expressing any resistance, confusion, stirrings, joy, or new resolve.

Fourth Reading—Contemplatio: Be still, resting in love.

Allow God's Spirit to work in yours.

—Scott Dewey

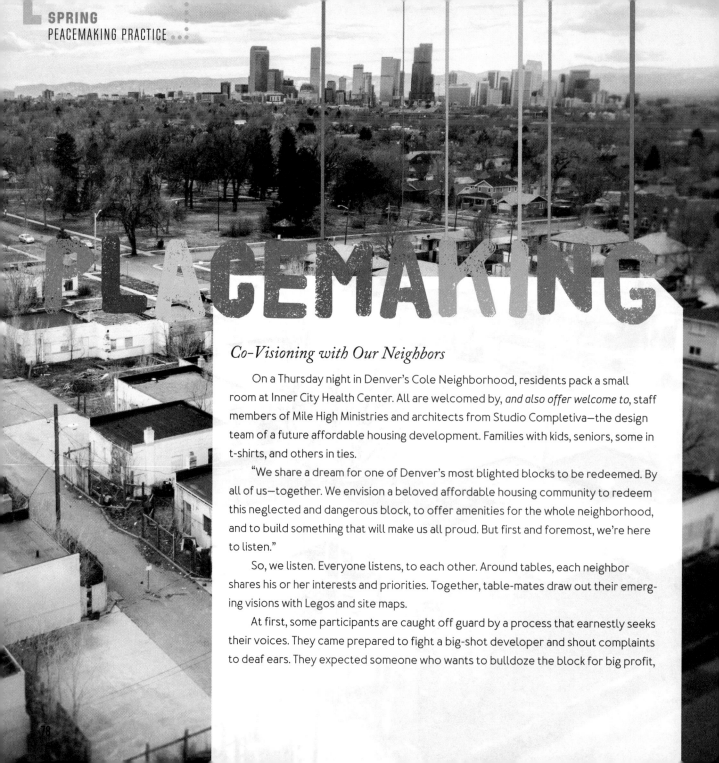

PLACEMAKING

Co-Visioning with Our Neighbors

On a Thursday night in Denver's Cole Neighborhood, residents pack a small room at Inner City Health Center. All are welcomed by, *and also offer welcome to*, staff members of Mile High Ministries and architects from Studio Completiva—the design team of a future affordable housing development. Families with kids, seniors, some in t-shirts, and others in ties.

"We share a dream for one of Denver's most blighted blocks to be redeemed. By all of us—together. We envision a beloved affordable housing community to redeem this neglected and dangerous block, to offer amenities for the whole neighborhood, and to build something that will make us all proud. But first and foremost, we're here to listen."

So, we listen. Everyone listens, to each other. Around tables, each neighbor shares his or her interests and priorities. Together, table-mates draw out their emerging visions with Legos and site maps.

At first, some participants are caught off guard by a process that earnestly seeks their voices. They came prepared to fight a big-shot developer and shout complaints to deaf ears. They expected someone who wants to bulldoze the block for big profit, and with good cause. These meetings happen around the city regularly, as required by the City of Denver. Developers must spend one meeting addressing local concerns before rezoning property. One short gathering for plans to be explained, for local voices to sound off, and for concerns to be addressed.

In our rapidly changing city, longtime residents of newly "hot" communities such as Cole, Five Points, and the North Side (Highlands) feel like they are in the front seat of Elitch's Mind Eraser rollercoaster: "Please keep your hands and feet inside of the ride at all times," the management instructs.

"We'd rather not," the disrupted neighbors say, and the kicking and screaming begins. You can read about it in the newspapers and follow along on social media, #mycommunityisnotforsale. In such a climate, developers typically enlist lawyers to navigate their projects around neighborhood opposition, meeting minimum requirements for engagement.

But this night, as participants explore ideas aloud, enthusiasm grows. Danny dreams of bees and birds and bicycles. Tahlia wants local, affordable, high-quality childcare for her son. Ellie, a new neighbor, envisions economic opportunity and retail in a mixed-use model. Sandy, who can remember a time when the block was flourishing, speaks of loving homes full of neighborly interaction. Mother Loretta nods.

Our project team itself is spurred by neighborly aspiration. Two generations of Johnsens—Jeff and his son Levi—have lived for decades in their home nearby, concerned and prayerful about the violence and crime this distressed property attracts. Our lead architect lives a few blocks away.

Far from seeing the Cole neighbors' participation as an obstacle, we see them as the cornerstone of Clara Brown Commons.[*] They have know-how, wisdom, and dreams that will drive the project. Their ownership is the lifeforce of the vision. They embody the social fabric that we as community developers seek to support. Chantel, Lawrence, Don, and their families are rightfully the dreamers of their own destiny and leaders in our Placemaking process.

—*Rebecca Mendoza Nunziato*

[*]*To read about Clara Brown, who is the inspiration for this affordable housing project, please see page 44.*

GENEROSITY
Life Overflowing

As a child, my sister and I would always fight over who got to write the check for the offering at church on Sunday mornings. Before we left the house, my parents would get out their checkbook and one of us would fill in the blanks before my parents would sign it. It was a subtle, but effective, way of teaching us about generosity. I always thought, "WOW, that is so much money to give away."

Every year my mom bought wrapping paper from neighborhood students raising money for field trips, and my dad regularly supported nonprofits and often wore T-shirts from public radio stations or Native American groups to prove it. They volunteered formally for service projects and informally by helping friends move, shoveling snow for an elderly neighbor, or visiting people in the hospital. I saw from a young age that giving was important—budgeting our time and money with others in mind was a strong family value.

My upbringing certainly has influenced my vocational path. And now, as I start having children, I deeply desire that my own family will carry on the sacrificial, humble, and joyful generosity I have seen in others.

Generosity is often misunderstood as something that occurs from those who are wealthy for those who are poor, but my work at the Justice and Mercy Legal Aid Center (JAMLAC) has turned the tables on this misconception.

Particularly, I think of the Gomez-Guerrero family. Initially, what stood out to me about their family was that they came through our doors as a married couple, which is highly unusual for clients at JAMLAC. Our clients are typically single women and moms, or occasionally a single dad, since we work primarily with victims of domestic violence.

Or maybe what struck me was their warm smiles, even in difficult circumstances. Either way, it is their generosity that continually stands out to me about this family. In my role as JAMLAC's development director, I meet with donors of all backgrounds who make it possible for us to serve poor and oppressed populations. Remembering their names and faces is important. But it is a truly special experience when the donors I recognize are also past clients.

The first time the Gomez-Guerrero family made a donation, they handed $300 in cash to Tina, our immigration attorney. Tina had been working on their immigration case for years, and they finally received their Green Cards (permanent residency status). They wanted to thank Tina and JAMLAC for changing their lives.

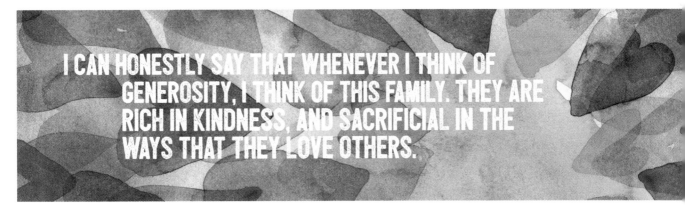

I CAN HONESTLY SAY THAT WHENEVER I THINK OF GENEROSITY, I THINK OF THIS FAMILY. THEY ARE RICH IN KINDNESS, AND SACRIFICIAL IN THE WAYS THAT THEY LOVE OTHERS.

The second time they donated, they brought the whole family and asked our receptionist to call me downstairs to receive the donation. As always, they were humble, full of smiles, and deeply happy that they were able to give back!

It seems as if every time they experience a financial blessing, they think of JAMLAC. They know firsthand how the money is used to transform the lives of victims and of undocumented immigrants. My own conversations with this family are limited—they only feel comfortable speaking Spanish—but it is always a pleasure to see them. They have expanded my view of giving, and they rightfully have shattered the paradigm of rich and poor.

I can honestly say that whenever I think of generosity, I think of this family. They are rich in kindness, and sacrificial in the ways that they love others. They have been donating for six years now, and we are so grateful that they are part of our JAMLAC community.

Both my parents and the Gomez-Guerrero family are inspirational givers, each in their unique ways. They have taught me that all of us can live out our faith and values through giving to others.

In my own personal journey, I struggle to model my life after these incredible examples. I hate to admit it, but I'm a worrier, and my giving tends to be influenced by fear of scarcity more than I wish—rather than by a celebration of abundance. In his Sermon on the Mount, Jesus encourages

> I HATE TO ADMIT IT, BUT I'M A WORRIER, AND MY GIVING TENDS TO BE INFLUENCED BY FEAR OF SCARCITY MORE THAN I WISH—RATHER THAN BY A CELEBRATION OF ABUNDANCE.

us not to worry about where our food will come from, about the clothes we wear, or what we have stored up. This reminds me that giving is an opportunity to be transformed.

I have found that I am at my best when I am giving. When I think about what I get to give, instead of trying to determine the bare minimum of giving, I am energized and aligned with my faith and values. I start to let go of "me-centered" concerns such as my future, my family, my food, or my time. I am thankful for my vocation in fundraising because I love inviting people into this experience of giving. I personally know the challenges, but also know the experience of overcoming fear. Our donors' generosity provides life-changing services to our clients, and it also brings each of us closer to the overflowing life of Jesus.

—*Nikki Koster*

Richer by Giving

Ministry is, first of all,
receiving God's blessing
from those to whom
we minister.

What is this blessing?
It is a glimpse
of the face of God.

You won't become poorer,
you will become richer
by giving.

We can confidently declare
with the Apostle Paul,
"You will be enriched
in every way
by your giving."

Those who need money
and those who can give money
meet on the common ground
of God's love.[1]

—Henri Nouwen

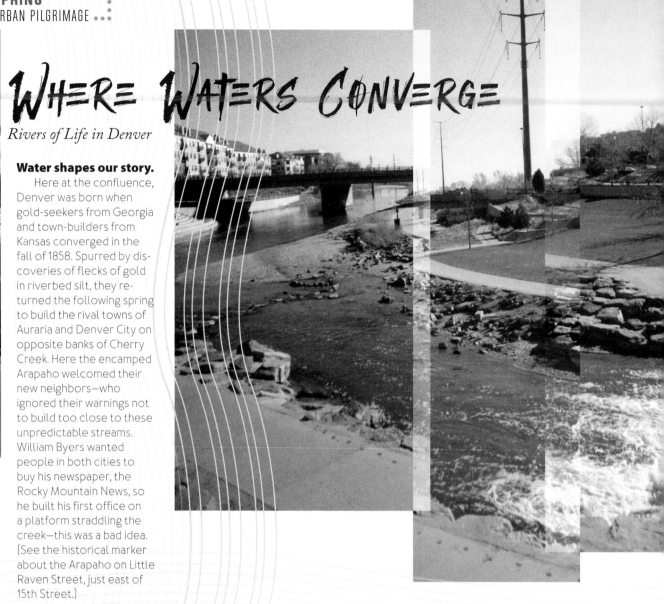

WHERE WATERS CONVERGE

Rivers of Life in Denver

Water shapes our story.

Here at the confluence, Denver was born when gold-seekers from Georgia and town-builders from Kansas converged in the fall of 1858. Spurred by discoveries of flecks of gold in riverbed silt, they returned the following spring to build the rival towns of Auraria and Denver City on opposite banks of Cherry Creek. Here the encamped Arapaho welcomed their new neighbors—who ignored their warnings not to build too close to these unpredictable streams. William Byers wanted people in both cities to buy his newspaper, the Rocky Mountain News, so he built his first office on a platform straddling the creek—this was a bad idea. [See the historical marker about the Arapaho on Little Raven Street, just east of 15th Street.]

As more waves of newcomers arrived, immigrant communities took turns getting a toehold in the young city at its lowest point—where sewage collected downstream, especially before indoor plumbing arrived in 1872. Some of our poorest neighbors still camp nearby, while much wealthier neighbors build spectacular lofts.

Reflect: *What problems and promise exist when the poor and the wealthy share spaces such as these?*

Water is wild.

For ancient peoples, including scripture writers, water often symbolized a chaotic and malevolent force. This imagery might seem foreign in the high plains of Denver, but our feisty little Cherry Creek flooded in the spring of 1864—killing at least a dozen people and carrying away many historic structures.

The South Platte has raged as well. When Colorado's typical annual rainfall came down in just three hours on June 16, 1965, the river exploded from its normal flow of 174 cubic feet per second to over 40,000, unleashing a deadly torrent through the city (including the spot from which I am writing these words—then, the Spa Motor Inn, which is now Joshua Station).

A hundred years ago, Mayor Speer led the effort to build a walled channel for Cherry Creek, giving it more room to safely vent its occasional fury. The Army Corps of Engineers later built Cherry Creek and Chatfield Reservoirs to store water and protect the city from flooding. Give thanks for forward-thinking government leaders and the many skilled professionals whose work makes our city safer.

Water is precious.

Water is particularly precious in our Denver climate. Only fifteen inches of rainwater falls on our city most years—plus 55 inches of snow, melting into another 5.5 inches of water. Two-thirds of Colorado's flowing water leaves the state; downstream communities have legal claim to most of "our" pure Rocky Mountain water. The vast majority of remaining water is used for agriculture, giving life to us through our food.

Of course, we city folk use water, too. The average metro Denver resident uses about 80 gallons of water each day. Does that number surprise you? It is one of the lowest rates of any major city in the west, and thanks to individual and collaborative efforts, per-person use is declining. Denver Water, our local utility, has an ambitious target for us of 30 gallons per day. Si se puede!

In case you're curious, lawn sprinklers use half our residential water. Toilets, showers, washing machines, faucets and leaks combine to cover most of the other

half. Denver Water also supplies nearly twenty thousand fire hydrants. Consider: Our water is perhaps as clean as any modern human community has ever enjoyed. "We flush much cleaner water than most people have to drink," my friend recently observed. Give thanks for the gift of water and spend time thinking about the value of this precious resource.

Water can be restored.

At a cost! Denver Water is developing a recycling system that could provide drinking water for 43,000 households when complete.

Meanwhile, like many rivers in urban areas, the South Platte has suffered from neglect and industrial waste. Within a hundred years after Denver's founding, our city's river was nearly dead by the 1970s. For over a generation now, The Greenway Foundation has been cleaning the South Platte, restoring verdant places for wildlife to thrive and for kids of all ages to have adventures—including Confluence Park. Denver Zoo uses mostly recycled water, and numerous others are providing similar leadership. Consider watershed restoration as a "spiritual" ministry—a way of loving God by loving people,

In the end, we will conserve only what we love; we will love only what we understand; and we will understand only what we are taught.[1]

—*Baba Dioum, Senegalese forestry engineer*

and loving people by caring for the places where they live.

Water is life.

Yes, water is a precious resource for physical life, and so much more—Jesus spoke of being "born of water and the spirit," illustrating what happens when we open ourselves up to be filled by God. "If you knew the generosity of God and who I am, you would be asking me for a drink, and I would give you fresh, living water... an artesian spring within, gushing fountains of endless life."

How are you experiencing that inner wellspring? What practices help you become open to the flow?

Water converges.

Perhaps confluence and convergence can be life-giving words for this "watershed moment" in these times too often characterized by divergence and division. Reflect on simple ways that you see people in our city coming together across demographic or philosophical boundaries for practical expressions of building healthy, beautiful communities.

—*Jeff Johnsen*

Pilgrimage Prayer

End your time at Confluence Park with a prayer such as this one. If the weather is nice and and the water level safe, consider wading—or at least dipping your hands into the water—as you pray:

Generous God, Fountain of Endless Life,

What a good and glorious place this is!

Thank you for the flowing waterways that are the veins of
   our city.

Thank you for clean water — essential to the life and vitality
   of our bodies.

Thank you for the living water that your Spirit brings to our
   innermost selves.

Water our dry and weary hearts with a shared vision for life
   and peace within the community that shares our watershed. Give us opportunities to express your generosity by
   caring for our waters, and extending clean water to those
   in need.

Amen.

BEN
LINDSEY

Ben Lindsey and Emily Griffith

Caring for Children in our City

A Denver municipal judge finishes his last day in office, loads files from his cabinets into his car, and drives away. He has an errand to run. Shortly, he will commit a profound act of civil disobedience.

Stopping at the edge of town at 13th Avenue and Umatilla, the soon-to-be-former judge unloads his files from the car into a ditch. Heaped on the pile are legal records of every defendant who has ever appeared before him in court. In front of a small group of newspaper reporters he invited, he sets the documents ablaze. A career is finished, official court documents go up in smoke, and justice for many will be preserved.

That judge was Benjamin Lindsey—a Denver street saint whose compassion led him to seek innovative approaches to pressing social problems, especially with juvenile criminal sentencing. At the turn of the 20th century, children in Colorado were tried and incarcerated no differently than adults. Courts sometimes sent them to "hard time" in harsh adult work camps, where they were traumatized and abused.

In 1902, Judge Lindsey had a "conversion experience" that set him on a course of change. After sentencing a boy to jail for theft, Ben heard the anguished cries of the boy's mother outside the courtroom. The bailiff told him that the boy had stolen coal to keep his impoverished family warm. The thought of punishing a child for doing something out of desperation to help his family survive undid Judge Lindsey. He had undergone the most powerful of human experiences—when an encounter with beauty or pain opens new ways of seeing.

From that time forward, Ben Lindsey became an advocate for Denver's youth. Ben began to take nighttime walking tours through Denver's poorest neighborhoods, deeply moved by the people that he met. Father Greg Boyle, a Jesuit priest who in our own time works with gang-involved youth, asks, "What if we stood in awe at the burdens people are able to carry, rather than in judgement of the way they carry them?"[1] Ben, whose job was judgement, took the initiative to stand personally in the midst of the lives of his defendants, feel their burdens, and advocate on their behalf.

This heart transformation led Ben to create one of the first juvenile courts in the country in 1903. As Denver's "Kids' Judge," he oversaw the court for over two decades. For Ben, justice was a matter of restoration—making things right—rather than simply a question of punishment. He led the charge to reform state laws that had created hardships for dependents of inmates, and he instituted a fledgling probation system as a pushback against the mass incarceration of non-violent offenders.

Beyond the courtroom, Ben organized and raised money for the construction of playgrounds and health spas in Denver. He was a leader in the national movement to abolish child labor. He wrote a best-selling book in 1910, *The Beast*, about corruption within city political machines—making him nationally known and

"THIS HEART TRANSFORMATION LED BEN TO CREATE ONE OF THE FIRST JUVENILE COURTS IN THE COUNTRY... JUSTICE WAS A MATTER OF RESTORATION— MAKING THINGS RIGHT—RATHER THAN SIMPLY A QUESTION OF PUNISHMENT."

leading to election reform. Will Rogers, the biggest celebrity of the 1920s, said that after George Washington and Abraham Lincoln, Ben Lindsey was his favorite American hero. One prominent reporter said, "Not even Francis of Assisi was more pure of life."

So what was he doing burning public files on his last day in office? Isn't that illegal? Certainly.

Judge Lindsey had run afoul of the Ku Klux Klan, who ruled Denver politics for much of the 1920s. As a result, he lost his job in 1926, was falsely accused of corruption, and was disbarred. When he left the juvenile court, he was concerned that his files might be used against all those defendants—now adults—who had appeared before him during 23 years as

EMILY GRIFFITH

Denver's Kids' Judge. Rather than let the documents fall into the hands of a Klan-sponsored judge, he destroyed them, putting his own career and legacy in jeopardy to erase the sins of young citizens and preserve their chance for a redemptive future. Ben moved to California after his "grace bonfire" to avoid recrimination.

Denver teacher Emily Griffith was the Kids' Judge's contemporary. She moved to Denver in 1894, when the city was in its worst economic depression and Ben Lindsey was just finishing law school. Living on Denver's West Side (the 1200 block of Lipan Street), Emily got a job teaching at the 24th Street School in Five Points, on Denver's East Side.

Emily's students were poor. Like Ben, she took her own walking tours of Denver slums, "surveying the ruins"—like the biblical figure Nehemiah in a devastated Jerusalem.[2] Her intention was to see the homes and lives of the children from her classroom. She became deeply concerned about the many immigrant and poor adults she met who had received no education. She started teaching night classes for anyone who wanted to study, regardless of age, race, gender, or background. Later, she would turn those night classes into the Opportunity School.

Emily became a teacher in Denver's public schools—after lying about her age on her application, for reasons that remain a mystery. She was 27 years old, but posed as a brand new 15-year-old teacher! Emily rose through the ranks, becoming Deputy State Superintendent of Schools in 1904, around the time Ben was developing the juvenile court. She continued to walk the poorest neighborhoods of the city, visiting students in their homes. Emily spent much of her income on streetcar tickets and food for her students. She visited them when they were sick, and worked with the police and Judge Lindsey when they got in trouble with the law.

Along with her personal investment and advocacy, Emily began to ask broad questions about why people experience poverty. Was there something defective about them as individuals, or was there a defect in the system that made it vastly more difficult for some groups of people to succeed in the marketplace? Emily concluded that the root of poverty is not simply lack of money, but a lack of education, hope, and a social network connected to economic opportunity. She intended, through the Opportunity School she founded in 1916, to help people get an education upon which they could build a more hopeful life.

When Emily retired in 1933, 100,000 students had attended her school, which became known as Emily Griffith Opportunity School. Now two million students later, Emily Griffith Technical College—affiliated with Denver Public Schools and the Colorado Community College System—provides more than two dozen career tech training programs for a tremendously diverse student body on three campuses. Along with the Lindsey-Flanigan Courthouse, these Denver landmarks remind us of how creative and compassionate change-makers can move the dial, personally and systemically, to foster practical ways of living more justly and joyfully with our neighbors.

These two transformative street saints moved beyond simple charity, to renewing the basic communal structures through which we share life in our city.

Blessed are you Emily Griffith and Ben Lindsey, peacemakers and children of God; thanks

CREATIVE AND COMPASSIONATE CHANGE-MAKERS CAN MOVE THE DIAL, PERSONALLY AND SYSTEMICALLY, TO FOSTER PRACTICAL WAYS OF LIVING MORE JUSTLY AND JOYFULLY WITH OUR NEIGHBORS.

to your labor of love, Denver children who have been "doomed to misfortune" (Isaiah 65) are given the opportunity to thrive, to play in peace, and to enjoy the fruit of their labors. Amen.

—*Jeff Johnsen*

CESAR CHAVEZ DAY

Sí Se Puede!

*Sí Se Puede!** As a phrase born out of fasting and prayer, it energized and united exploited farmworkers across the nation.

When Delores Huerta and Cesar Chavez chose *Sí Se Puede* in 1972 as the rallying cry for their movement, the United Farm Workers Union was gaining momentum through strikes and boycotts.

How could poor field workers so successfully stand up to consumer demand for artificially cheap produce, profiteering, and embedded racism throughout much of agribusiness—and demand rights?

They embodied a strange sort of power and leadership, "from below." It's a Moses-like story: a declaration of freedom for captives, mobilization of slaves, and an unshakable trust in God's presence not only in the waiting but also in the wading into the sea, into the unknown.

Chavez and his fellow organizers pressed into the painful, risky, and sacrificial struggle.

He led "spiritual fasts"—

at one point nearly starving to death after 25 days. He led a 340-mile march to Sacramento in grueling heat, carrying the image of Our Lady of Guadalupe— a sacred symbol of motherly devotion, divine intervention, and holy pilgrimage. Such faith-filled actions inspire and invite us into the power of a humble, vulnerable God as we face injustice today. Our loving struggle for shalom can only be sustained with such a combination of deep spirituality and courageous action.

Still today, when you join the Chavez Day March in North Denver, you'll hear *Sí Se Puede* as a song welling up from the streets—an affirmation of faith.

—Rebecca Mendoza Nunziato

Sí Se Puede is most commonly translated as "Yes we can!" However, the Spanish language offers a unique ability to phrase something beyond "We can" or "you can" or "I can"—rather, it allows for a universal phrasing and could be translated as "it can be done" or "it will be."

Awakening to Grace

Springtime at Mile High WorkShop

> Forget your perfect offering
> There is a crack, a crack in everything
> That's how the light gets in
> —*Leonard Cohen*

Making my way through piles of furniture and fixtures to the back of a warehouse, I find myself musing, *what a strange place.* On the far end of Bud's Warehouse[1], a whole world opens up to me. Wood shavings scent the air, mountains of pillow-making materials press against plastic walls, and

sewing machines hum in harmony. This is no ordinary job site.

Tattooed workers smile and welcome me into their workspaces. I get the impression they enjoy their jobs, and take pride in their respective crafts. These employees are hired by Mile High WorkShop, a job training social enterprise for community members rebuilding from addiction, homelessness, and incarceration.

One employee catches my eye. I've never seen a seamstress at work. Her hands guide each stitch, her feet tap the control pedal in syncopated rhythm. Joannie looks natural, entranced in her trade.

Joannie will be on her way soon, I learn—graduating from the WorkShop program and entering the outside workforce as a skilled technician. She, like dozens of her peers, has experienced the springtime of her life in this warehouse.

Joannie has faced many cruel winters that

brought her to this moment. She came to the WorkShop after years of struggle with substance abuse. Her addictions led her in and out of abusive relationships, and she became a single, struggling mom at a young age. The continuing challenge of sobriety left her to the legal system—incarcerated and losing custody of her precious daughters. She experienced all the disappointment and regret you could imagine from such a time. Locked up and alone, she was unable to overcome mounting obstacles to survival, let alone self-sufficiency.

I can't help thinking, *this is enough to crush a person*. Ten times over. So many in our city are unable to recover from these harsh realities.

Like every new trainee of the WorkShop, Joannie chose a skill—product fulfillment, woodworking, or sewing. For the first time, Joannie partnered with a social worker and a job coach to hone a craft and to craft her future. This wasn't the usual dead-end, minimum-wage job; she could sense that immediately. She felt something she hadn't in a long time—grace.

Anne Lamott observes that "the movement of grace is what changes us, heals us, and heals our world. Grace finds us exactly where we are, but it doesn't leave us where it found us. It helps us breathe again and again, and gives us back to ourselves...."[2]

Grace is the first invitation of transfor-

GRACE IS THE FIRST INVITATION OF TRANSFORMATION. AS A GIFT WE CANNOT CREATE OF OUR OWN WILL OR RESOURCES.

mation. As a gift we cannot create of our own will or resources, it beckons each of us sojourners toward the beauty of surrender. It is the life impulse of each breath of each living being—be it behind bars or between breaststrokes at the rec center. Grace is in the buzz of the WorkShop's power tools and the practical interconnectedness of a production team.

At the WorkShop I am reminded that grace simply awaits our awareness—ready at any moment to sweep us up in the flow of God. Grace must be the surprising warmth I feel radiating from these concrete floors and metal roof in the back of a warehouse.

Daily, the WorkShop team reads aloud their shared values, as a spoken litany of healing and change:

Growing Everyday: *We are diligent in becoming the best version of ourselves.*

Responsible to Each Other: *We succeed as a team and continually strive to build trust.*

Acting with Integrity: *We are honest and reliable in our interactions*

Community of Peace: *We cultivate a love-filled space with compassion and respect for all.*

Excellence in Our Work: *Whether with people or products, we seek quality outcomes.*

Team members speak up in turn, sharing their tangible experiences of grace on the job. Joannie is a beautiful embodiment of such transformation through grace, of a life loved forth into blossoms of purpose. On her first day in the sew shop, Joannie remembers, she simply traced a line in stitches on a piece of paper. Her anxiety began to calm as she progressed through the day. Confidence was cultivated day by day in the program.

This renewal translated to Joannie's family life. Back in the courtroom, the judge could now see a stable woman ready to reunite with her children. You know that feeling of warm sun on your face after a long winter? The elation of green grass poking through the frost? Then you've glimpsed a speck of the redemption we saw when Joannie's family embraced each other that day.

Amid the rhythm of the sewing machine, Joannie was exposed to rhythms of encouragement and growth in the WorkShop community. She found herself surrounded with the support she needed to face each day, and herself. This community of peace held Joannie together on the hard days—when addiction and old patterns were triggered, and fear weighed cold and heavy on her shoulders.

At the heart of transformation is the gift of stumbling, yet trusting our worthiness. Alongside Joannie I face my own self in the mirror each day, wondering if I can trust the Springtime: will the birds cease their singing tomorrow? Will I ever stop feeling so wobbly and frail? I wonder how hibernating creatures can trust their instincts and awaken with anticipation.

Little things become evidence of the

abundance, richness, and energy are everywhere around Denver these days.

Get out into summer! Experience the Cherry Creek Arts festival for free—our city's signature celebration of the visual, culinary, and performing arts. Wander into the Dragon Boat Festival on Sloan's Lake, spread out a picnic blanket at an outdoor concert, graze the farmers' markets, and meander through First Friday art walks. Don a costume for Comic Con (make mine Marvel!) and take a culinary tour of the Taste of Colorado in Civic Center Park.

Every neighborhood experiences growth these days, from luxury quarters in Cherry Creek, to tiny home villages and desperately-needed affordable housing projects. Colfax Avenue, the longest commercial street in the U.S., is remaking itself all the way from Aurora westward to Golden. Growth and expansion are the energies of both summer and Denver today. Amid all the complications of a growing city, we can welcome the season of warmth with jubilation!

—*Scott Jenkins*

There is a festival in the Christian tradition that falls early each summer and carries the twin themes of growth and diversity. Pentecost celebrates these related gifts, reminding us of the outpouring of the Spirit's energy in marvelous diversity, available to all. Denver's explosive growth, while benefiting some, brings great difficulty and displacement for many of our most vulnerable neighbors. We pray that God will enlarge our hearts to act with compassion, extend hospitality, and support public policies that create an environment of peace and welcome for a growing and diverse population.

Decades ago, Denver was a stopping place before the arduous trek over the Rockies for travelers headed west. Today we are a destination for those wanting to put down roots and call our city "home." We sit at the base of some of the most beautiful mountains in the world, at the doorstep of the fertile Great Plains. May our beloved city reflect values that will benefit all who call this place their own.

O Beloved Creator whose Spirit burns within us,
may this season with its long hot days
stir us to fun-filled activities with those we love.

STIR US BY YOUR FIRE

May our passion for your life expressed in us
bring hope to those in need,
engagement with the struggle for justice,
and a renewed energy as we work for peace.

As the lengthening of days opens life
to more time spent outdoors,
may our eyes be opened to your presence—
speaking to us through our natural world.

O Beloved Creator,
transform us by your Spirit's fire within.
Amen.

—Scott Jenkins

help me love

A Prayer from
1 Corinthians 13

O God, O Christ my Brother, help me love the people around me more than the sound of my own voice. Help me to love, more than trying to be entertaining.

O God, O Christ my Brother, so much of me gets caught up in trying to know everything, especially the powerful stuff. I confess that much of the time I'd rather move mountains than simply love. I get so caught up in wanting people to see my great sacrifices that I forget to care for who they really are.

O God, O Christ my Brother, help me to be patient— as you are. Help me to be kind. Help me toss out the envious, possessive parts of me. Help me quit looking for feedback that would justify my own grandiosity.

O God, O Christ my Brother, I often am rude to others; help me quit that. And what's with this "one-up-manship" that tickles me so much? My temper gets out of hand so quickly, Lord. Convict me of the grudges I hold; help me let them go. Why do I take such pleasure in rehashing others' shortcomings? I want to feel your joy when others have cool breakthroughs.

O God, O Christ my Brother, I want to grow into a love that is enduring. I want to find roots that inspire fresh trust. I want a perspective filled with unfading hope. I want confidence in your love that outlasts anything. I want to love without fail.

—John Hicks

God's Loving Friendship

This prayerful adaptation of the Apostle Paul's familiar treatise on love comes from our friend and colleague, John Hicks. For four decades, John has companioned the poor in Denver—particularly chronically mentally ill, homeless adults. He pastored a small church on Capitol Hill, St. James Urban Church, and directed The Network, a coffeehouse dubbed by many "the living room of Christ." Network's only program is to welcome people in from the streets and build long-term, redemptive relationships. And, play lots of chess!

John also has companioned many of us who are not poor, including urban activists who are always at risk of spinning out of control in our fervor to right the world's wrongs. He was one of the first to invite our Mile High Ministries team to a contemplative way of praying—modeling a practice he referred to simply as "staring at God."

John captures something important about the contemplative path when he says, "I may be one of the few people I know who actually believes that God likes me." Contemplative spirituality invites us to sit in friendship with reality as it is in front of us, including people as they really are—and sometimes most challenging, ourselves as we really are. This provides the foundation for John's open, vulnerable prayer. Secure in God's loving friendship with me, I can then confess the ways I miss the mark of the loving, Christ-like person I wish to become—knowing that nothing can diminish how much God likes me!

—*Jeff Johnsen*

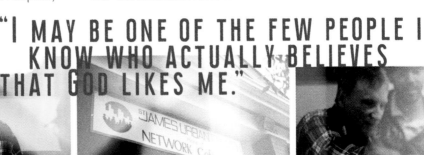

"I MAY BE ONE OF THE FEW PEOPLE I KNOW WHO ACTUALLY BELIEVES THAT GOD LIKES ME."

OPENING OURSELVES TO THE WORD

For the word of God is alive and powerful. It is sharper than the sharpest two-edged sword, cutting between soul and spirit, between joint and marrow. It exposes our innermost thoughts and desires.
—Hebrews 4:12

I am drawn to the practice of integrating scripture into my life by engaging with it in silence, in the presence of God. I experience in scripture the living breath of God moving into my soul. When I was a child, I was encouraged to read and pray. I could feel in my bones and in my very being that God had given me a gift as I read. It spoke to me of my identity rooted in God.

The discipline of slowing down with scripture helps me give full attention to God. I am nourished by the Word and led deeper into the fullness of my life. My struggles, my joys, mundane everyday happenings, and the created world speak to me and become ways of connection. As I have grown through quiet prayer practices, I find I can connect with God at any time or place.

Ruth Haley Barton, in her book *Sacred Rhythms,* says, "When we engage the scriptures for spiritual transformation we engage not only our mind but also our heart, our emotions, our body, our curiosity, our imaginations, and our will. We open ourselves to a deeper level of understanding and insight that grows out of and leads us deeper into our personal relationship with the One behind the text. It is in the context of relational intimacy that real life change takes place."[1]

SITTING WITH SCRIPTURE

1. Sit in a quiet place. Choose a portion of scripture for reflection—a verse or a passage. If you are new to scripture, possibilities might be Psalm 23 (a poem about God as our shepherd), Matthew 5:1-13 (blessings of Jesus), or 1 Corinthians 13 (a chapter about love).

2. Open your heart to God's presence and voice within your heart. "Be still and know that I am God" (Psalm 46:10). Express thanks for the fullness of who God is. In a listening posture, as you are prompted in your spirit, pray for others—perhaps friends who come to mind, or those who are in need.

3. Enter a time of *Examen* (personal examination). What is my deepest soul cry? What do I trust to be true about God? What is most deeply true about me? Open yourself to the full mercy and intimacy of God.

4. Turn now to the written word. Slowly read your chosen portion of scripture three times. Between readings, meditate on the written words. Think about what is being impressed upon you. What might God be saying to you? What do you need to know about God, yourself, or others in this moment? How should you respond to what you have been shown today?

5. Sit fully enveloped in the presence of God. Trust God to be God, and recognize that this is more than enough.

—*Sandy Lee, with Penny Salazar-Phillips*

When Better Isn't Best

Once upon a time, a generous volunteer family created a fabulous Christmas party for our Joshua Station families. Correctly assuming that many of our kids, moms, and dads—in their experience of homelessness—had never been invited to a lavish holiday dinner, they spared no expense or effort. Our community room positively gleamed

The Lame Summer Picnic

with tableware, centerpieces, and lights. A piano was carried in for entertainment, servers sported top hats and gloves, and the room was decked with holly.

As the hour drew close, our staff grew nervous—on behalf of the volunteers. After all their effort, would our residents show up? Staff began knocking door-to-door, pleading with families to come. Some weren't sure how they'd fit the scene, wondering if they had the right attire. Others came and enjoyed the food but didn't linger.

Another time, a generous volunteer group planned a fabulous picnic for Joshua Station residents to kick off summer. Colorful flyers announced the event. As the hour drew near, our staff grew nervous. Had anybody heard from the volunteers lately? Nope. Disappointment sank in as families waited around and stomachs growled.

Then a most amazing thing happened: someone ran out for hotdogs, a dad brought ketchup packets from his room. Half-full bags of chips showed up. Bread, soda pop, cookies, and cake emerged from resident rooms. Too much to eat!

Forever after, it was the best meal anyone could remember.

Reflect: How empowering is our excellence in service? Who has the joy of giving? Whose effort is celebrated? Who are the heroes?

—Scott Dewey

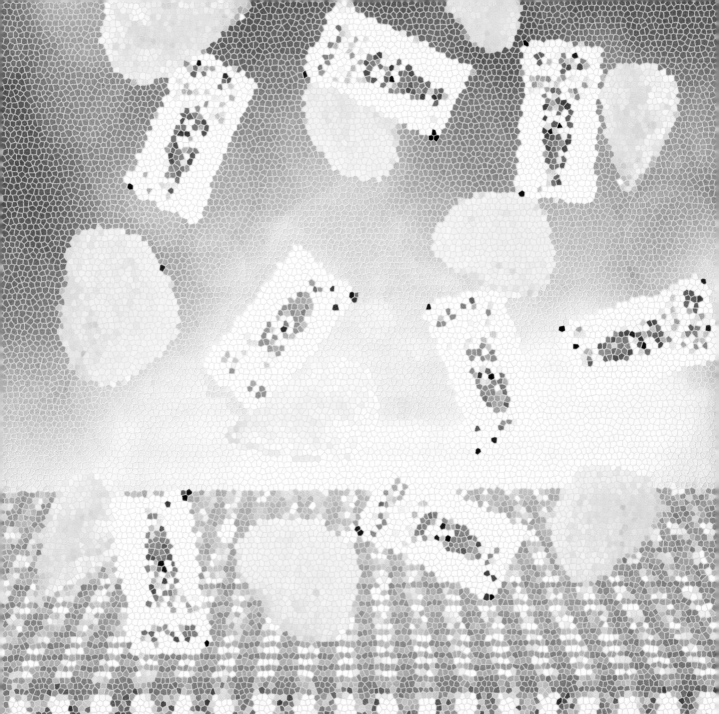

JUSTICE AND SHALOM
A Path of Peacemaking

What does the Lord require of you but to do justice, and to love mercy, and to walk humbly with your God?
—**Micah 6:8**

Sitting on the steps of an old house on Denver's Capitol Hill, deep in conversation with my friend, mentor, and co-laborer Jeff Johnsen, I took my first mental steps toward seeking justice for people struggling with poverty and oppression. As youth minister at Bear Valley Church in the suburb of Lakewood, Colorado, I had sensed God calling me to "defend the cause of the poor and needy" (Jeremiah 22:16). Talking with Jeff prompted me to action.

With no idea where the path would lead, I was compelled to walk forward anyway. My family and I, along with some other friends, moved into a northeast Denver neighborhood in the 90s when it wasn't so cool to do so—a beautiful, vibrant part of the city that was also challenged with poverty and surging gang violence. People experiencing oppression became my friends and neighbors. These rich relationships led me to a place I had never imagined in my wildest dreams—law school. Of course, the legal profession is a great venue for seeking justice, but law was a totally new world.

Twenty-five years later, I sometimes shake my head at where this path has led. Along the way, in 2006, a dream of mine was realized in founding the Justice and Mercy Legal Aid Center—a faith-based, non-profit law firm that provides full-service legal representation for victims of daily hardship and cruelty. A wonderful team of full-time attorneys, paralegals, interns, and volunteers now manage approximately 50 active cases each week for indigent clients.

Names have been changed to protect clients.

From Church Sanctuary to the Courtroom

It didn't take me long to realize that the courthouse is a significant place in which to minister. Outside any courtroom are people looking like "sheep without a shepherd," to quote the lament of Jesus. Denver's City and County Building and the newer Lindsey Flanigan Courthouse are beautiful from the outside—true landmarks in our great city. Inside, hundreds of folks interact with a confusing and scary system with specific rules, enforced by serious people in black robes. The majority of our clients are victims of domestic violence, for whom the lost and overwhelming feeling is especially acute. Not only are they in an unfamiliar context, they are in dispute with someone of whom they are deathly afraid.

What is justice for these very vulnerable people, often women and children? My experience has shown me that justice is an elusive concept. Former Supreme Court Justice Potter Stewart once famously remarked on another topic, "I know it when I see it." That said, it can help to take a closer look at justice's many facets, which I'll do here through the lens of our faith.

Justice in the Bible

Scripture has served as a light for my journey. Many Bible passages exhort us to "do justice," or "seek justice," or "administer true justice." But how? It is helpful to understand two polar opposite concepts portrayed in scripture's pages:

First, *oppression*. When a scripture passage refers to the poor, it most often identifies the cause of their poverty as oppression. Lowell Noble, in his book *From Oppression to Jubilee Justice*,[1] describes oppression as "the unwarranted, unfair, and sometimes unintentional use of wealth, power, or position which deprives the poor, powerless, or disenfranchised of basic needs and rights." Gary Haugen, founder of International Justice Mission,

says injustice is "the abuse of power to take from others good things that God intended for them (life, liberty, dignity, fruit of labor)."[2] Oppression is the reality we face daily with our clients.

Second, *shalom*. Shalom is a state of peace and blessing which recognizes the inherent dignity and worth of each person. It allows people to meet their own needs, while contributing to others. Shalom is a rich and multifaceted concept, with an expansive vision of right relationship with God, one's family and friends, the larger community, and world. It requires an even playing field (equity), adequate prosperity for human flourishing, and healthy interdependence. To experience shalom is to thrive and to experience the image of God in all of life.

At JAMLAC we seek justice by helping people move from a place of oppression, where they experience injustice, to a place of shalom, a place of thriving. We work to build bridges from the one reality to the other, through the civil legal system. Our clients come to us feeling powerless and afraid, searching for help and hope. Yet they are strong! They are resilient and beautiful. Often we help them see dignity and strength within themselves.

Each day this bridge-building work is a *ministry of presence*. Together with legal expertise, we bring our desire to *be with* our clients not only as advocates but also as fellow sojourners in life. We walk with them and learn from them as they grow stronger, find their voice, and become productive members of the larger community. As we journey with them toward shalom, we find ourselves also profoundly transformed by the partnership.

A Woman's Journey Toward Justice

Shannary was brought to the United States from Cambodia by San, a man she had met online. He too was from Cambodia but had built a long and successful career in the U.S. A few days after her arrival on a fiancé visa, as they were making wedding plans, she was presented with a legal document written in English—a pre-nuptial agreement. San took her to his lawyer's office and had her sign it in front of a notary. The document was not explained to her, except that it was necessary for her to sign it in order to get married.

Soon after their marriage, Shannary began to experience abuse, control, and manipulation. Despite it all, she sought to be a faithful and loving wife, and they had two children together. Eventually, she could no longer endure the abuse, and sought help. She was referred to JAMLAC by one of our collaborating organizations, the Asia Pacific Development Center.

It was not until our first court appearance that I was made aware of the pre-nuptial agreement. She had not thought about it since the day she signed it. I'll never forget the look of shock on her face and her tears as I explained to her that this pre-nuptial stated that in the event of divorce, she would get nothing. We did not know what would happen for Shannary and her children.

In the end, at a contested hearing, we were able to convince the court that the pre-nuptial agreement was invalid—as it was signed without knowledge

BUT EACH OF US CAN "DO JUSTICE" IN ANY CONTEXT.

of its content and consequences. Shannary would receive resources from the marriage that she had helped to acquire. She would be able to take care of her children and move forward as a productive member of society.

We "did justice"—built a bridge from oppression toward shalom—together, in partnership. Shannary was strong and brave, creating a pathway for a better future for her family. We do this work every day at JAMLAC in the venue of the civil legal system. *But each of us can "do justice" in any context.* Helping vulnerable people find mental or physical healthcare, meaningful employment, or sustainable housing is doing justice. Walking with people overcoming addictions is doing justice. Building friendships across barriers is doing justice. And that is truly "what is good and what the Lord requires of us."

—Steve Thompson

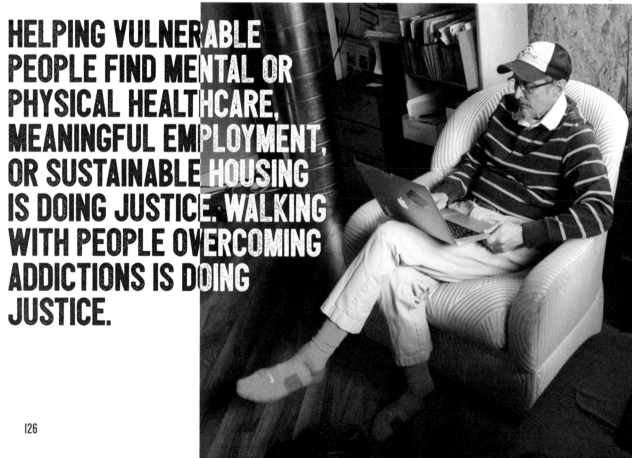

HELPING VULNERABLE PEOPLE FIND MENTAL OR PHYSICAL HEALTHCARE, MEANINGFUL EMPLOYMENT, OR SUSTAINABLE HOUSING IS DOING JUSTICE. WALKING WITH PEOPLE OVERCOMING ADDICTIONS IS DOING JUSTICE.

FIRST RESIDENTS

A Journey of Remembrance

GRIEF
MEMORIZES THIS GRASS.
RAW
COURAGE,
     BELIEVE IT,
RED—EYED AND URGENT,
STALKING DENVER

—*Simon J. Ortiz, from "Sand Creek"*

Pain is hard to face. But summer, in its fiery nature, invites us to pay attention to all that is illuminated.

In our journey at Mile High Ministries we have leaned into the fullness of stories entrusted to us: beautiful moments of redemption and tender wounds of trauma. We have learned that stories are grounded in physical places—captured in the walls of our homes, the pews in which we sit, the parks where we play—whether we recognize it or not.

We honor Denver places—some well-loved, and others with hard realities. Places of pain can be difficult to find, as though we have been eager to erase our darkest moments from public memory. Hard places are likewise difficult to engage, requiring inner work that calls forth maturity and vulnerability.

Contemplative tools provide guidance for facing such darkness. Ceremonies such as funerals, public litanies of remembrance, and our own community's Liturgy of Sacred Sight (page 244) are vessels for carrying pain with integrity. So too, pilgrimage—an intentional spiritual journey toward the sacred—invites us to love our city more fully by uncovering and tending her unhealed wounds.

Here, we offer a brief pilgrimage around Denver's Civic Center Park, to help us hold sacred the memory of this land's original inhabitants. (Adapted from Stephen Leonard's and Thomas Noel's book, *A Short History of Denver*.)[2]

We know, though not fully enough, that Denver is home to this history:

Within a few short years after the Gold Rush gave birth to Denver, Arapaho and Cheyenne people were driven from this watershed and surrounding plains, deprived of their livelihood, stricken with new diseases for which they had no immunity, killed by United States armies, and driven onto resource-poor reservations.

In November of 1864 at Sand Creek, 650 of Colonel Chivington's Colorado Volunteers ambushed an encampment of unsuspecting Native Americans. Over 150 people were murdered; mostly women, children, and elderly—while the young men were away hunting. Chivington's men killed the wounded, mutilated the corpses, and set fire to the village before announcing victory to Denver and the nation—parading body parts through the city streets. These atrocities were initially celebrated as a battle of the American Indian Wars and only later condemned widely as a massacre.

If you are new to this story of displacement and ethnic cleansing, you'll want to do a bit of background reading about Cheyenne and Arapaho, as well as the Sand Creek Massacre.

May we grow to hold both our city's beauty and pain in our hearts without becoming overwhelmed and turning away.

—*Jeff Johnsen, with Rebecca Mendoza Nunziato*

Begin on the east side of the Colorado State Capitol at Preston Powers's bronze statue "The Closing Era," which, "true to the nineteenth-century view that Native Americans were fated to vanish, depicts the intertwined demise of the Indians and the bison." Note how this statue was relegated to the rear of the building. *Reflect: what if Powers's work was displayed next to the war memorabilia on the front steps? Would it prompt us to wrestle with the competing narratives?*

Next, walk to the west side of the capitol, locate the 1909 monument honoring the Civil War dead which refers to the Sand Creek "battle." At its base, find the name of Silas Soule, who was murdered for refusing direct orders to lead his troops into the slaughter of Native families. Also find the plaque placed in 1999, which refers to the Sand Creek "massacre." *Reflect on how we select words in retelling stories.*

At the northwest corner of Colfax and Broadway, artist Frederick MacMonnies had proposed a memorial remembering the region's Indians. Instead, in 1911, city fathers had the monument crowned with a statue of Christopher "Kit" Carson. Carson is a troubling

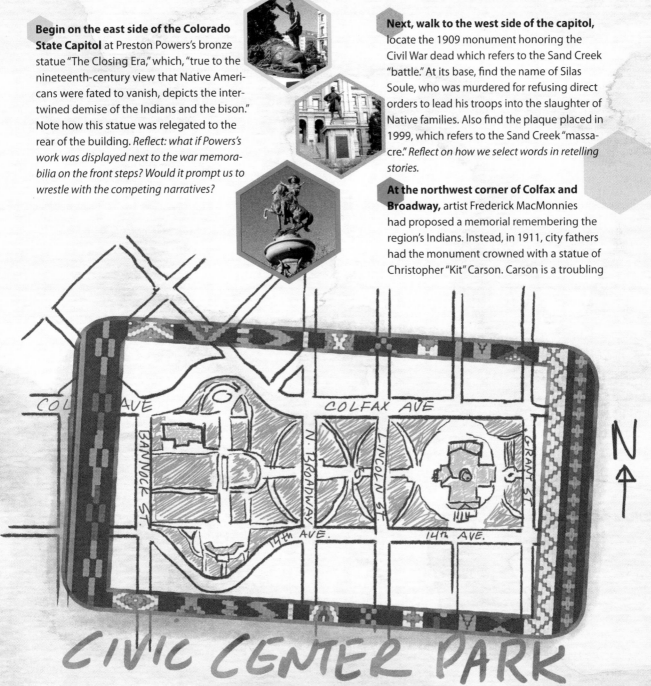

CIVIC CENTER PARK

129

figure who led numerous acts of violence against America's indigenous peoples, including the tragic "Long Walk" expulsion of the Navajo from Canyon de Chelly and other parts of their homeland. *How does public art inform our collective conscience?*

Cross Colfax and enter Civic Center Park. Denver historians Stephen Leonard and Thomas Noel ask us to consider "what percentage of the homeless people lingering there might be Native Americans whose ancestors called all of northeastern Colorado home before 1861." *Reflect on the turn of events for people whose long heritage is tied to this land now being forbidden from sleeping on state and city property.*

Just north of the center of the park, stop at the modern statue of Christopher Columbus. Colorado was the first state to honor Columbus with a holiday in 1907, but after decades of peaceful protest led by the American Indian Movement, Denver renamed the day Indigenous Peoples Day in 2016. *Consider what it means to honor the explorer who paved the way for the violent conquest of the hemisphere's indigenous peoples.*

Nearby stands Denver artist Alexander Phimister Proctor's 1922 bronze statue "On the Warpath," a romantic view of the plains Indians. *Reflect: might this depict a view Euro-Americans could embrace only once native people had been removed from the land?*

Just south of the park, across 14th Avenue, head inside the Denver Public Library and visit the Western History and Genealogy department on the fifth floor. Ask a librarian for an original copy of the study commissioned by the US Congress condemning the Sand Creek Massacre. Also ask to see Silas Soule's original letter to Edward Wynkoop detailing the atrocities. Plan a time to visit nearby Denver Art Museum when they feature exhibits of native art. *Think about your own education about Native Americans—what did it include? Exclude?*

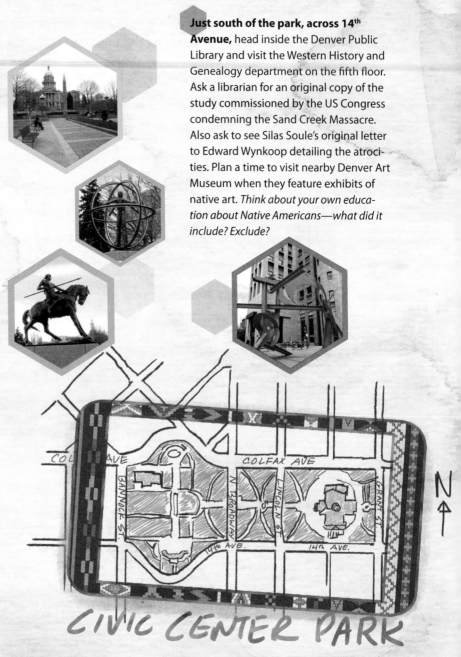

CIVIC CENTER PARK

Near the intersection of 14th and Bannock, pause at the northeast corner of the Ponti-Sudler building. Here once stood "Wheel," an art installment by Edgar Heap of Birds, an Arapaho-Cheyenne artist. Ten red metal trees displayed inscriptions such as "Bison Life Ends Rez Life Begins 160 Acres Plow and Poverty," "Gold Wars Starve Suffer," and "NAH-KEV-HO-EYEA-ZIM—We are always returning home again." Another sign informed homeless people, including Native Americans, of a city ordinance prohibiting them from sheltering there. "Police will expel them as their ancestors were expelled more than 150 years ago," write Leonard and Noel. To see this piece of art, however, you may have to wait. It was removed for museum expansion. After protests and negotiations with the artist, there are plans for "Wheel" to be reinstalled in a nearby location. *Reflect: Displaced yet again?*

For the next location, you might wish to travel the 2.5 miles to the southwest corner of 8th Avenue and Vallejo Street, where a small monument marks the former location of Camp Weld, a military camp. Here in 1864, tribal leaders met Governor John Evans and US army officers in an overture of peace. The "Camp Weld Council" conversation went poorly, leading directly to tragic events two months later: it was from this spot that the 3rd Colorado Volunteers marched to Sand Creek and returned home after the massacre, falsely proclaiming their military victory. *Imagine what our state would be like had these peace talks been successful.*

Yingna Cai / Shutterstock.com

Finally, please consider taking a day or a full weekend to visit the Sand Creek National Historic Site, 180 miles southeast of Camp Weld. *Be prepared to be moved, informed, and deeply troubled by what you experience here.*

Courtesy National Park Service

131

Carolyn Finnell and Corky Gonzales

Galilee People

Theologian Virgilio Elizondo points toward what he calls the Galilee Principle at the heart of Christian scripture: those whom the powers overlook hold profound, if hidden, significance in God's economy.[1] Galilee was a marginalized, ethnically-mixed hinterland. The incarnation of Christ as a Galilean carpenter embodied redemption for an oppressed people group and a fallen human race. In the same way, marginalized "Galilean people" are often instrumental in redeeming the "Jerusalem people"—in other words, insiders nearer the center of the social order.

Carolyn Finnell's life could be "exhibit one" for Elizondo's Galilean Principle. Carolyn had cerebral palsy, a neurological disorder that interferes with the brain's ability to control voluntary movements of the body. "My body is a parable of the Christian church," she would joke, "The head knows what to do, but somehow the body isn't getting the message!"

Carolyn was a gang member—of sorts. She was one of the "Gang of 19" who, on July 5 and 6, 1978, rolled their wheelchairs into the busy intersection of Colfax and Broadway in what may have been the nation's first demonstration for wheelchair-accessible public transportation. Chanting "we will ride," they blocked traffic until they got

arrested. The Denver jail wasn't accessible, ironically, and since they could not be incarcerated, they were released. They promptly rolled right back over to the intersection to re-create their human chain. Their protest eventually led to accessible public transportation in Denver and across the nation.

As a young woman in the 1960s, Carolyn was sent to a nursing home. "I wasn't sick or old, but nursing homes were the only public housing option at the time for people with disabilities." Although nursing homes were expensive to run, federal policy would not allow disabled people who received assistance to live on their own. Carolyn joined a class action suit demanding a policy change. After ten difficult years, while being denied medical treatment for a serious and painful medical condition, Carolyn and her friends won the right to live independently.

It was only the beginning. Throughout the 1970s and 80s Carolyn and friends, called the Atlantis Community, traveled the country to advocate for basic opportunities. Hundreds of newspaper clippings—now covering the Atlantis "Wall of Fame" on Cherokee Street—tell the story. "To boldly go where all others have gone before!" was their slogan. The civil rights movement that began with the Gang of 19 ultimately resulted in the Americans With Disabilities Act of 1990. Carolyn is remembered as "one of the most articulate and intellectual" advocates of the movement.

"We were a motley crew," remembered Carolyn of her fellow protesters, who were often arrested during their protests. After the 1978 demonstration in Denver, someone wrote an editorial in the Rocky Mountain News complaining that the protesters were poorly dressed and unkempt. "It's true," says Carolyn, "Atlantis made

"ATLANTIS MADE A POINT OF USING THE LOSERS OF THE DISABILITY WORLD, AND IT WAS US LOSERS WHO CHANGED THE WORLD!"

a point of using the losers of the disability world, and it was us losers who changed the world!"

"God chose the foolish things of the world to shame the wise," wrote the Apostle Paul. "God chose the weak things of the world to shame the strong."[2] Carolyn served on the board of Hope Communities, which provides quality affordable housing in Denver; she was an elder in her Baker neighborhood church; and she led a community called TRYAD (To Reconcile You, Able-bodied and Disabled)—eventually opening a hospitality house on Capitol Hill that provided an alternative to the lonely isolation experienced by many people with disabilities.

Before her death in 2006, Carolyn told me about a time after leaving the nursing home when she decided to take a roll around the lake at Washington Park by herself—a journey that took her several hours. Struck by the beauty of

CORKY"
GONZALES

the park and the sun's reflection on the water, she was overwhelmed by the sense of freedom and adventure. "To be sure, there was some danger. If my chair had slipped on the path, I would have fallen into the lake and drowned. It gave me a thrill! I was responsible for my own life—finally! Suddenly, I was glad I was disabled—that, at the age of 29, I could be completely turned on by a trip around the lake. Sometimes I feel sorry for able-bodied people who need so much to keep them entertained."

As Carolyn Finnell and her Atlantis "gang" demonstrated, sometimes the redemptive work of "Galilee people" necessitates disruption. That was certainly true of Rodolfo "Corky" Gonzales who, like Carolyn, rooted activism in a spiritual vision.[3] Corky—nicknamed because as a kid he was always "popping off" like a cork—was a Denver eastsider, graduating from Manual High School when he was just 16, despite working the fields with his family during the Great Depression. He first made his name as a professional boxer, retiring at age 27 with an impressive record of wins.

In a remarkable pivot, Corky came to national prominence in 1967 as the author of an epic poem, "Yo soy Joaquín" ("I Am Joaquín"). The poem rooted a social agenda within a cosmic vision. Joaquín is the voice of Chicano people—second-generation Mexican-Americans who by virtue of their deep history and complex identities were neither fully Indian nor European, Mexican, nor American—claiming their right to "Aztlán," an ancestral home that included the American southwest. The message of "Yo soy Joaquín" was not expressly a Christian vision, yet it resonates with Elizondo's Galilee Principle, inspiring Chicanos to change the world. The poem had a lightning impact on the social and political activism of the Chicano community.

Corky had become involved with politics a few years earlier, registering Latinos in various local and national elections. By 1967, however, he became disillusioned with the two-party system and founded the Crusade for Justice in Denver—first as a response to police brutality, and then to pursue economic, educational, and political self-determination for Chicanos and Mexicanos. In 1969 he convened the first-ever Chicano youth conference, a catalytic moment in the development of Chicano leaders. In 1971 he founded a dual-language private school, Escuela Tlatelolco, at 1571 Downing Street, next door to Crusade headquarters.

The most influential period for the Crusade ended in 1973 when a protest turned violent, leading to a gun battle and deadly explosion at the Downing Terrace apartments, next to Crusade headquarters. There are deep differences in the stories told about who initiated the violence—Crusade or the police. Corky continued to lead for three decades even after that crisis, though with a lower profile. The Denver Public Library honored Corky by naming the branch library at Colfax and Irving after him.

Since his death in 2005, Corky's legacy lives on in his family. Corky's daughter Nita led the school for decades, graduating hundreds of students and shaping a generation of young leaders before finally closing in 2017. Corky's son Rudy directs Servicios de la Raza, an influential Denver organization providing culturally responsive human services.

THE DENVER PUBLIC LIBRARY HONORED CORKY BY NAMING THE BRANCH LIBRARY AT COLFAX AND IRVING AFTER HIM.

Carolyn Finnell and Corky Gonzales—two of Denver's inspirational, creative, disruptive, and sometimes controversial leaders—died less than a year apart. Their impact continues to reverberate from our city out across the nation, pressing for genuine change in the world.

"Blessed are those who hunger and thirst for justice," Jesus said, "for they will be filled." Blessed are you, Carolyn and Corky, who led your "Galilee people" in creating a more just world for all of us!

—*Jeff Johnsen*

JUNETEENTH MUSIC FESTIVAL

Playground in the Streets

Juneteenth, a grand celebration in northeast Denver, invites us to experience a technicolored reality in shades of joy and hope. In the heat of summer, the city's historic Five Points neighborhood becomes a playground of art and culture, food and fanfare.

Juneteenth commemorates the belated June 19, 1865 announcement to Texas slaves of their emancipation, which had actually been decreed by President Lincoln two and a half years earlier. Our Denver parade, the biggest in the nation, dates to the 1950s when it spanned an extended weekend of marching, gospel music, and community fun. These days it's all packed into the third Saturday in June.

This Denver Holy Day flourishes as a sign of peacemaking. It recalls a historical moment that would warrant bitter complaint and recrimination—not only for centuries of enslavement on American soil, but the withholding of the very news that would set millions of people free. Yet here at 27th and Welton is a joyful high-stepping parade, shaved ice, and a soundstage with dancing into the night.

One way of seeing the world is through the lens of winners and losers—a battleground. As we grow in awareness of the complexity of ourselves, of one another, and of our city, we develop more expansive ways of seeing. What would it mean to imagine our city and our world instead as a playground where all may join hands, delighting in freedom? Each summer, Juneteenth provides an exuberant glimpse.

—*Rebecca Mendoza Nunziato*

Many women who experience domestic violence feel disconnected from reality, as if they are living a nightmare. Yesenia is no exception.

Yesenia carries herself with a quiet strength—so much so, that it might appear that she has recovered from the violence in her past. Yet I can see the pain in her eyes as we meet in one of our conference rooms. Slowly, she pours out details of the most horrific moments of her life.

Yesenia came to the Justice and Mercy Legal Aid Center (JAMLAC) three years ago, and has since been a beacon of hope for us all. Yesenia, now in her mid-20s, was born in a small town in Mexico. At the age of six, she became a protector for her younger brothers. "My fragile mind

From Terror to Strength

Yesenia's Story

and tiny body always had a plan to protect them when my alcoholic father would beat my mom," she recounts. "I used to wrap them in my arms and hide them underneath one of the only two beds we had."

Yesenia begins to cry, as the sun comes through the window, illuminating her face. Like so many victims who sit in this chair, vulnerable and afraid, her broken heart is exposed to me. Each of our team of victim advocates, paralegals, lawyers, and program staff will hold her fragile story with care.

"I still regret not being able to help my mom more—but I was so small. Why didn't I ever run outside screaming that my mom was being beaten? That she was being destroyed in the worst of ways? It still haunts me; the feeling of guilt lingers."

Eventually, pressing through fear, Yesenia's family managed to escape and migrate to the United States. Unfortunately, things went from bad to worse. At the age of 15, she was sexually assaulted. She then married at the age of 17, looking for the protection and safety she never received. This would be the beginning of years of physical and mental abuse. With tears, she recalls her then-husband's cruelty. "He constantly reminded me of how little I was worth as a person, how inferior I was because I was raped, and that I had no value as a woman."

Sadly, Yesenia's experience is not uncommon. On average in the

> AROUND 55% OF FEMALE HOMICIDE VICTIMS IN THE UNITED STATES ARE KILLED IN CONNECTION TO PARTNER VIOLENCE; THIS NUMBER INCREASES TO 61% FOR WOMEN OF HISPANIC DESCENT.

United States, 24 people per minute experience rape, physical violence, or stalking by an intimate partner—more than 12 million women and men over the course of a year.[1] In Colorado over 16,700 people reported one or more domestic violence crimes to Colorado law enforcement in 2014.[2] Many others have never contacted authorities. At JAMLAC over 80% of our clients identify as victims; we work to defend their rights and restore their dignity.

For Yesenia and hundreds of other JAMLAC clients, the challenge of domestic violence is complicated by their immigration status. Being undocumented, Yesenia was afraid to seek help or call the police. I can hear the fear in her voice even now as I listen to how alone she felt. Most immigrants do not know help is available, and far too few have the legal representation needed to protect their basic rights.

Yesenia felt like a prisoner in her own body, she recalls. "My tears were the only way to escape reality. I always thought that one day he would kill me. My two little babies, four and sixteen months old, were my biggest concern. Finally, the day I feared the most arrived. My only plan to save my children was to lock myself in the bathroom, where I had calculated a way to squeeze them through the window in order to save them. I hugged them with all the love and strength that a mother can wield. We cried together. I closed my eyes and prayed with them, waiting for my

> I ALWAYS THOUGHT THAT ONE DAY HE WOULD KILL ME. MY TWO LITTLE BABIES, FOUR AND SIXTEEN MONTHS OLD, WERE MY BIGGEST CONCERN.

death. I wondered if my death would be the only escape. And then, at that moment, I saw my own childhood reflected in my children's eyes. I realized that they were reliving my story, although I had desired a different childhood for them." Moments before her breaking point, her husband became frustrated because he couldn't get into the locked bathroom and left the house. She finally gathered the courage to call the police.

Yesenia is a survivor. Around 55% of female homicide victims in the United States are killed in connection to partner violence; this number increases to 61% for women of Hispanic descent.[3]

I feel overwhelmed as Yesenia tells me: "I know God heard my prayers because he directed me to JAMLAC. The staff opened my eyes to what was happening and gave me hope. JAMLAC was my advocate through divorce, a legal custody battle, and my immigration case. I don't know how to pay them back because this type of whole-life transformation does not have monetary value. But what I do know is that I don't want anybody to suffer what I suffered. My story has meaning if at least one person in the shadows of domestic violence hears it and seeks help."

As Yesenia gained strength, her engagement with life and the outside world changed profoundly. She started by volunteering at a local police station as a victim advocate, and working at a fast food restaurant to pay the bills. She eventually was hired as the victim intake coordinator at the

JAMLAC WAS MY ADVOCATE THROUGH DIVORCE, A LEGAL CUSTODY BATTLE, AND MY IMMIGRATION CASE.

local police station and is currently working on her social work degree. Yesenia hopes to attend law school someday, and help others in need.

Yesenia's life is an inspiration for all of us. We look into her eyes and know she is a renewed woman. We feel so honored to be a part of her story of transformation, and humbled by her gratitude. "I will do anything for this organization," she often tells us. "You are my family. For me, my children, and for many others who are still living in the shadows of domestic violence, Justice and Mercy Legal Aid Center is family."

—*Marlene Bedoya*

SHAKING THE SYSTEM
Awkward Activism

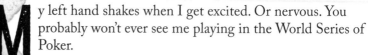

My left hand shakes when I get excited. Or nervous. You probably won't ever see me playing in the World Series of Poker.

My hand tremor is no big deal most of the time. But when I was handed a microphone at a protest rally in front of the federal courthouse and asked to read a statement for the television cameras… zap! Adrenaline shot through me and my hand shook so hard I could barely hold the mic.

I showed up to the event intending to simply be a face in the crowd. Religious leaders were asked to wear clerical collars to show that support for "DREAMers" (young adults brought to this country as children, without documentation) is rooted in our faith commitments. There was no reason for me to be nervous. The crowd was small, comprised mostly of friendly DREAMers who took a genuine risk to participate in a public event. Only one local TV station showed up. Yet there was my left hand, quaking like an aspen leaf in a summer breeze.

Being a protest spokesperson is not a natural role for me. I do want our society to be more just. But I'm a reluctant public activist, seeking change mostly through patient community development on a small scale. It doesn't help that I often see more than one side to the issues. And did I mention that my left hand shakes?

I switched the microphone to my comparatively stable right hand. That was no better, since the paper with the statement I was

> BEING A PROTEST SPOKESPERSON IS NOT A NATURAL ROLE FOR ME. I DO WANT OUR SOCIETY TO BE MORE JUST. BUT I'M A RELUCTANT PUBLIC ACTIVIST…

to read was now flopping around in my left hand.

I don't remember the words that I struggled to read at the courthouse event. I do remember that they included a quote from Charles Chaput, the conservative archbishop of the Roman Catholic Church in Denver at that time: "It is my hope, and that of many other people of faith, that our elected federal officials will find the courage in the months ahead to pass immigration reform and rethink enforcement tactics that tear families apart. In the end, the ultimate question for Congress—and for all Americans—is whether we want to live in a society that accepts the toil of migrants with one hand, and then treats them like criminals with the other."[1]

The following Sunday I preached in a large suburban church, on the gospel story about Jesus dining in the home of a tax collector named Levi. Apparently, this was a scandal in his time. How could Jesus be friendly with "sinners" and culturally impure outsiders? Some of the people Jesus enjoyed eating with habitually broke the law. Others bent it to enrich themselves at the expense of others. As a religious leader, wasn't Jesus concerned his presence might appear to condone their actions?

Jesus' joyful participation at Levi's dinner party offended every kind of social and religious norm upholding purity, good reputation, and an upright way of life. Jesus even untethered his good news from the capacity to stay on the right side of the law. At least, that's the conclusion I reached in my sermon.

In closing, I mentioned how inspired I had been by the courage of young immigrants at the recent rally. When I acknowledged that we serve undocumented people in our programs at Mile High Ministries, the room grew quiet. Had I miscalculated?

After the service, a line of people quickly formed to speak with me. One or two thanked me. Most gave me an earful; they wanted to make sure I understood that the DREAMers' cause is not, in fact, just—and that I should never have been at such a rally. One man threatened to call our board of directors and major donors, and to have Mile High Ministries shut down! Wanna guess what happened to my left hand in that moment?

I had hoped my church friends would appreciate that God's good news invites us to see all humans as created in God's image, and to stand with them as advocates when they are most vulnerable. In fact, I'm frequently moved by stories about people in Denver who have wealth, power, and status—and, frankly, very conservative political views—yet quietly give themselves to long-term personal relationships with people who are incarcerated, mentally ill, homeless, or undocumented. I'm also inspired by the willingness of some of my faith-driven friends to shake social and economic systems on behalf of vulnerable people.

My friend Michelle Warren is one of those brave system-shakers. Some years ago, she got good and mad about nudity on a strip club sign in the neighborhood where she was raising her children. Michelle got a petition going among neighbors calling for the sign to be changed or removed. She even met with Denver's mayor, who contributed to a fund to fix the sign. Minor changes got made to the sign, but Michelle emerged from the battle transformed. For one thing, she met her neighbors, some of whom she learned were undocumented immigrants and who shared more in common with Michelle than she had previously understood. She also gained vision for what happens when common folks begin to recognize their capacity to shape the future of their own communities.

And so it was that a few years later Michelle

invited diverse groups to march across the city in solidarity, and rallied a crowd outside a for-profit immigration detention center to pray for change and demand systemic reform.

In all of this, Michelle has patiently drawn reluctant activists like me into greater levels of engagement, convincing us of a seamless connection between worship, prayer, and challenging systems of power that lay heavy burdens upon our neighbors.

The Tuesday morning after my shaky

> MICHELLE HAS PATIENTLY DRAWN RELUCTANT ACTIVISTS LIKE ME INTO GREATER LEVELS OF ENGAGEMENT, CONVINCING US OF A CONNECTION BETWEEN WORSHIP, PRAYER, AND CHALLENGING SYSTEMS OF POWER.

corralled a bunch of us on a chilly winter day to march around the public space between the State Capitol and the City and County Building during rush hour, under a big banner reading "Evangelicals for Immigration Reform." Denver drivers seemed unsure about whether or not to honk, perhaps unsettled about whether they would be endorsing evangelicals or immigration reform.

On another occasion, Michelle organized 300 church people to walk silently for a mile down Colfax Avenue on a Sunday afternoon to kneel on the steps of the State Capitol, praying for peace and reconciliation between police and communities of color. Later she led a group onto the plaza of the Denver Justice Center to call for an end to mass incarceration that ravages our urban communities. Michelle has gathered us in church fellowship halls to pray for educational equity,

performances at the federal courthouse and at church, I drove to a Bible study that I attend weekly. Given what happened after my sermon, I thought about skipping that morning, since I knew a few men from the church would be there. As I walked into the room, I saw two of the older men in the group—who had both been present for my sermon—speaking in hushed tones as though sharing a secret that I was pretty sure was about me. I was considering turning around to leave, when they paused. "There he is now," said one. "Uh-oh," I thought, my old faithful left hand preparing to erupt. The other man stood, put a hand on my shoulder, looked me straight in the eye, and said; "Good job, buddy. We need to hear those kinds of things more often!"

If that's the case, this shaky-handed activist will keep awkwardly trying to shake the system.

—*Jeff Johnsen*

144

May the compassionate heart of God
fill that soulful place deep within,
moving us to see the broken and afflicted
in the ruins of their shattered dreams.

May we gaze upon those held in captivity by addiction,
materialism, or their own insatiable quest for power—
with the perceptive eyes of Jesus
and his liberating embrace.

Bring the Oil of Gladness

May our proclamation of the Lord's favor
be seen in our sacrificial deeds for others,
our collective resistance against self-indulgence,
and our questioning of all that oppresses.

May we comfort all who mourn,
even as we mourn what must die within us,
bringing the oil of gladness
upon the unfolding of our truest selves.

For the sake of the world,
for the sake of our children,
and their children.

Amen.

—*Scott Jenkins*

From Isaiah 61

The Spirit of the Sovereign Lord is on me, because the Lord has anointed me to proclaim good news to the poor… to bind up the brokenhearted, to proclaim freedom for the captives and release from darkness for the prisoners, to proclaim the year of the Lord's favor… to comfort all who mourn, and provide for those who grieve… to bestow on them a crown of beauty instead of ashes, the oil of joy instead of mourning, and a garment of praise instead of a spirit of despair.

Here is what we seek: a compassion that can stand in awe at what the poor have to carry rather than stand in judgment at how they carry it.

— *Gregory Boyle,* Tattoos on the Heart: The Power of Boundless Compassion

BEYOND OUR EFFORTS:
Transformation

> [*"...The magnificent enterprise that is God's work."*
> —Prayer of Oscar Romero]

Things change.

That's the good news.

Or the bad news, if you're invested in the status quo. I once heard a church history professor, toward the end of his life, give a talk to Denver church leaders about faith and society. Christian faith simply doesn't hold sway as in past times, he lamented—things we hold dear are slipping away. He called on us to staunchly resist the outgoing tide. An African-American pastor raised his hand, drew a long breath, and said softly to the white professor, "The good old days weren't so good for some of us."

I'm anxiously invested in the status quo, pacing the waiting room while doctors probe a loved one for a disease that could remove her from us. "Turns out everything's fine," I want the oncologist to come out and announce. I want the same faces in the family photo next Christmas.

We resist change, grieve change, hope for change, welcome change, and work for change—sometimes all at the same time. Oh that change might show the courtesy to proceed forth neatly organized! Change behaves badly. Change lurches and lunges, stutter-steps and sprints, while we cheer or gasp. Or it creeps beneath; one day we blink, bewildered. Who rewrote the rules and rendered useless our trusty tools?

We change. The inner whirl behaves no more politely than the whirl outside. Some changes we experience as falling. Others rising. Still others are too confusing to tell. Unmoored by change, we search for bearings. We winch down the anchor and hope it catches on known touchstones. We study change theory. Change toward what? For what? Why? How? We pull out old maps and compass, or we fiddle with the GPS. We scan the horizon for signs.

We resist change, grieve change, hope for change, welcome change, and work for change— sometimes all at the same time.

"No sign will be given to this generation," Jesus said, "except the sign of Jonah."[1] Sign of who?

There is an archetypal pattern in scripture narratives—in fact in universal human experience—of descent, desolation, and ascent. Joseph the favored son, thrown into a pit and into prison, eventually saves a nation. The nation he saves becomes enslaved in Egypt, wanders in the desert for a generation, and then becomes a world power. As a world power it is conquered and destroyed, exiled to Babylon, and later rebuilds. "I tell you the truth, unless a kernel of wheat falls to the ground and dies, it remains only a single seed," Jesus taught. "But if it dies, it produces many seeds."[2] Death, burial, and resurrection—the "paschal mystery." Faithful followers descend into the waters of baptism, are submerged, and are raised again to newness of life.

"For as Jonah was three days and three nights in the belly of the great fish, so the Son of Humanity will be three days and three nights in the heart of the earth."[3]

Jonah who? For Sunday-school students Jonah provides one of the many curiously quirky Bible tales, but hardly a candidate for MVP prophet or the great sign for an age. Becoming swallowed and suffocated is likewise hardly an alluring vision to proclaim.

Alluring or not, down we go.

Things fall.

Empires fall. Heroes fall.

Life falls apart. Plans fail. Marriages fail. Health fails.

Water falls, and pools in the lowest places.

Blood of the fallen also pools. After violence, firehoses get most of it off the sidewalk. A group of us quietly gathers in such places to reflect, but we don't have much company for our ceremonies. Not to blame anyone for that; none of us is inclined to linger long in the lowest places.

Golden ash leaves flutter onto my keyboard as I type in October, but dark green oak leaves cling tight overhead. In a few weeks they'll turn crimson with determination to hang on. December snows will howl, acorns will drop, but those oak leaves on my yard tree will still flap like tattered brown battle flags. Sub-zero January nights pry them loose, but not without a fight.

Reflexively we resist falling. Panicked by vertigo, we grab for hand-holds. "Now my soul is greatly troubled," Jesus said, after he shared his wisdom about the falling grains of wheat. It's one thing to talk about the archetypal experience of all humanity—which he was—and quite

No wonder, then, that we invest so much determined effort to avoid our experience and awareness of falling!

another thing to face it personally and immediately—which he also was. Sliding toward the abyss, he sweat drops of blood.

No wonder, then, that we invest so much determined effort to avoid our experience and awareness of falling! Binge-watching a TV series sure beats sweating drops of blood, I'm here to confirm. My own sun-splashed city virtually defines itself by a high culture of recreation, which carries a wealth of physical, social, and psychological benefits important to me. Including: being readily available for numbing and diversion.

At some point such efforts fail. One day, or likely one night, we find ourselves overcome and overwhelmed; swallowed whole. We strain to hold together, but the sinews of our psyche shred. "My God, my God," gasped the psalmist—and Jesus—*in extremis.* The *dark night,* St. John of the Cross called it—the terrible passage of the senses and ultimately of the soul into the abyss.

French activist and mystic philosopher Simone Weil explored the depths of *malheur*—translated commonly as "affliction." Though often occasioned by hard experiences, affliction for Weil is distinguished from suffering by the level of disintegration it entails. We humans possess a noble and amazing capacity to "buck up" and endure under suffering. In affliction, however, one's entire being loses its very capacity to remain whole, integral. We come apart. Weil calls it a "pulverization" by the "mechanical brutality of circumstances."[4]

In affliction, even our meaning-making capacity for language fails: "As for those who have been struck the kind of blow which leaves the victim writhing on the ground like a half-crushed worm, they have no words to describe what is happening to them. Among the people they meet, those who have never had contact with affliction in its true sense can

> In affliction, however, one's entire being loses its very capacity to remain whole, integral. We come apart.

have no idea of what it is, even though they may know much suffering.... A kind of horror submerges the whole soul."[5]

While much of religious and cultural life works diligently to avoid such horror, the wisest spiritual formation prepares us to undergo it. Simone Weil, St. John of the Cross—and others whose gift to the world was their attention to the soul—teach us that the soul's journey through darkness is, in fact, absolutely essential.

After a particular trauma during a season of traumas, I am sitting with my therapist. Words fail; mine and hers. Scarcely little remains even to feel. After silence, she is saying something about caterpillars turning into butterflies, which unnerves me, as normally she is not given to saccharine clichés. I'm not ready to hear this at all, though I can summon no strength to protest. "It liquifies." I do hear *this*, and suddenly she has my attention. "It completely disintegrates inside the chrysalis, losing all form and structure whatsoever. No tissue remains. There is no caterpillar changing into a butterfly. There is neither one; only DNA soup—held together by something outside of itself, but nothing within itself."

I have no idea, as I listen, about the biological accuracy of this—but I know it depicts a clear mirror image of myself in this moment. Over the course of the hour I remember—I barely remember, but I do remember; I know; yes I remember that I know—that I am held. Held not from within where nothing holds, but from without, until whatever is without form and void within can be reconstituted in the love that has always moved over the surface of the deep of my life. I cannot discern any reconstitution now. From past experience I know it will require time without a timetable.

In utter darkness we survive longer than we imagine possible, but not indefinitely.

I have spoken of the darkest night: the night of winter solstice, we might say. In utter darkness we survive longer than we imagine possible, but not indefinitely. We simply cannot fully adapt to such harsh conditions, though as poet Theodore Roethke says, "In a dark time, the eye begins to see."[6] In *Learning to Walk in the Dark*,[7] Barbara Brown Taylor reminds of the great importance not only of night but also of *twilight*. Twilight precedes and follows darkness—and links it to day. In dim light we are uncertain, but this very uncertainty provides possibilities for necessary transformation.

This *liminality* (an in-between "threshold" space, to borrow from Victor Turner's anthropology) and *disorienting dilemma* (from Jack Mezirow's transformative learning theory) is a fundamental condition for human transformation—personal, relational, or societal. We may grow incrementally for a season without dis-integration, as the caterpillar does, and such growth is good. But transformation toward qualitatively new levels of wholeness and beauty never happens without disruption.

We emerge a wet mess with puzzling, useless wings we don't recognize. We are vomited forth from the great beast onto a distant shore. Whatever the metaphor, to our surprise we discover ourselves alive. Exhaustion slowly gives way to attentiveness; we notice how the red wounds become scabbed, and in turn the scabs yield pink scars. We experience strange new itches, intuitions, curiosities, and stirrings. Gingerly we flex and stretch. Vulnerable, we risk. When we hurt, the old darkness does not overwhelm us. We find new kindred spirits, and trust old companions in deeper ways. Days lengthen, sap rises: Spring. What pushes up from the moist and enriched black earth "will produce many seeds" when the sun blazes.

> Transformation toward qualitatively new levels of wholeness and beauty never happens without disruption.

The sign of Jonah: orientation, disorientation, reorientation. Life, death, resurrection.

Over the long sacred journey of the soul we learn to trust, and find the pattern of seasons themselves to be trustworthy and reassuring. We can be present to the beautiful moment or the chaotic hard moment with equal authenticity and integrity. We can respond more appropriately to what each invites of us. We can embrace the dark angels of failure and loss as our teachers. We can find lavish beauty in unlikely places and celebrate with giddy abandon. We can allow ourselves to be "in the flow" of life with decreasing addiction to control, and increasing capacity for interconnection and community. As leaders within communities, organizations, churches, businesses, government, or families, we learn to recognize these change patterns and grow into our roles for stewarding transformation.

It is "the magnificent enterprise that is God's work"—the great unfolding of love, to which we are so graciously invited.

—*Scott Dewey*

> We can find lavish beauty in unlikely places and celebrate with giddy abandon.

Autumn

BEYOND OUR EFFORTS

CELEBRATING Autumn

Beauty in life—beauty in
  death,
arm in arm so close here.
Song of golden aspen, red
  maple, orange oak.
Graceful dance of falling
  leaves.
Distant whisper calling
  birds to come away.

Bountiful harvest blessing.
Bright pumpkin faces.
Canning gifts shared.
Celebrate apple sauce and
  salsa.
Laughter, awe, and mercy
  holding hands.
—Penny Salazar Phillips

ENTERING A TIME OF HARVEST AND REFLECTION

Now we turn our gaze toward autumn, which is without a doubt my favorite season. More than any other season, autumn is a time of remembering. It speaks of what is calling from the depth of earth and soul.

Personally, I find it hard to embrace the mysteries of dying that characterize this season. Yet, it re-shapes my soul like no other time of the year. I ask myself: how is it that letting go and dying to self could be a thing of breathtaking beauty? I feel part of an ancient call that has been answered by generation after generation.

I can easily engage this splendor while gazing at the leaves turning to release their greenness. Our city becomes an array of color, rivaling any artist's palette.

Fall can remind us of the imperma-nence of everything. As it approaches, we recall the budding of life in spring and the flowerings of summer. Now, in fall, the leaves drop, and bare branches remind us of the fleeting nature of all things.

It is said that autumn is a laborer that works with the maturing sun to bring bountiful harvests. In its progression, autumn acts as a gleaner that decomposes summer flowers and produce.

This is also a rich season spiritually. Fall encompasses the Christian commemoration of All Saints Day and the Jewish celebrations of New Year and The Day of Atonement. These reflective times are ripe with the opportunity for remembering and renewal. What is it we need to release? Where do we need to begin anew? Where, in this vulnerability, is breathtaking beauty?

During the introspective aspects of this season, we look towards the harvest. In this harvest season, I invite you to gather with friends and family and weave lasting memories into your tapestry. Consider many activities that celebrate harvest in our city:

◆ Explore the aspen, oak, and maple in our Denver neighborhoods and in the nearby hills. Breathe in their color and give thanks. Come walk the labyrinth at Mile High Ministries, listening to the still, small voice of God.

◆ All ages delight in Arvada's Festival of Scarecrows, in the pumpkin harvest and Día de los Muertos, and in Joshua Station's own Trunk-or-Treat.

◆ All you artists who revel in visual and cinematic creativity, visit the Denver Film Festival, Denver Arts Week, or CineLatino.

◆ For those who savor the fruits of the vine and the gifts of the brewmasters, tasting abounds at the Denver Beer Fest, the Great American Beer Festival, the Denver International Wine Festival, and Denver Oktoberfest.

As we enjoy the gifts of this season, we reflect on the bounty in our own lives. The world is ripe for reflection as the air cools and the leaves crunch beneath our feet.

—Penny Salazar Phillips

May We Love Lavishly

Creator of the sun and moon, we raise our voice to you.
We pray, Great Spirit, that in our journey through life
We may know the harmony and rhythm of the setting sun.
We pour out our deep-seated gratitude . . .
For the bountiful harvest your hand has provided,
For the beauty of the dying leaves,
For our surrendering and our letting go,
For those who have gone ahead.

We seek your forgiving mercy and your vast grace.
We look for your image in all we meet.
We pursue your image in deepest center.
We pray that we may look longingly toward the twilights of
    our lives.
With open hands and hearts may we be blessed like the
    brilliance of the sunset.
Enlarge our hearts that you may enter in, O most Holy
    Trinity . . .
May we feel your greatness; may we answer your call; may
    we love lavishly.
Hallelujah, Hallelujah, Hallelujah!

—Penny Salazar Phillips

Letting Go

"Have the same mindset as Christ Jesus:
who, precisely because he was in the form of God
he did not consider being equal with God grounds for grasping;
on the contrary, he poured himself out
by taking the very nature of a servant,
by being made in human likeness."[1]

Philippians 4:5-7

Abundance in Emptiness

Yellow, orange, red. Dying leaves fluttering through the breeze. Raked into piles. Pressed into earth.

These same leaves are most *alive* in the radiant heat of summer, chlorophyll rushing through their veins.

Yet, ask any Coloradan: when is nature most vibrant, the most awe-inspiring? *September!*

In fall, tourists and locals alike rush upward, to higher elevations, to witness the golden wave wash across the peaks of the Rockies: artists and poets wade in the aspen groves, families capture annual portraits, and the elks' mating calls echo in the evenings.

For the leaves, it is in the falling—detaching—that they are most beautiful. They break into pieces and sink into the earth, offering themselves back to the cycle of life—a transformation unlike any other.

This autumnal spectacle reflects a concept the mystics know well: *Kenosis.*

Kenosis describes Jesus' way of being in Philippians 2:7—emptying himself, letting go in humility. Like the autumn leaves, death reveals the fullness of life.

Cynthia Bourgeault writes of this mystery as a "path of descent." While many spiritual seekers imagine that the way to God is up, she points to Jesus' example of becoming "nothing" as the deeper reality:

Everything can be embraced, but the catch is to cling to nothing. You let it go. You go through life like a knife goes through a done cake, picking up nothing, clinging to nothing, sticking to nothing. And grounded in that fundamental chastity of your being, you can then throw yourself out, pour yourself out, being able to give it all back, even giving back life itself. That's the kenotic path in a nutshell. Very, very simple. It only costs everything.[2]

This beautiful, jaw-dropping image of love is an explosion of abundance and generosity, a profound gift to us humans, so addicted to our earthly treasures, our self-image and our ladder-climbing.

We think it is in our summery green days that we are at our best—winning promotions or raising honor roll students. Yet Jesus' message subverts this logic. He invites us into the depths of emptiness, and into the discovery of where love truly lies. It is only here that we are not threatened by the risk of letting go. Beatrice Bruteau calls this a "sacred liberation":

When you are perfectly empty of all predicates… then you are intensely full of pure "I am." And just as this point is reached, it explodes into the creative outpouring energy, "May all of you be and be abundantly!"[3]

This fall, we invite the wisdom of our brothers and sisters, the Quaking Aspen, to teach us the way of Jesus and invite us downward, towards our truest selves, towards the earth below—trusting that love will carry us into all goodness in this season of harvest.

—Rebecca Mendoza Nunziato

THE JESUS PRAYER
Abundant Mercy

"Lord Jesus Christ, Son of God, have mercy on me, a sinner."

This simple phrase, an ancient prayer from 4th century Christian monastic communities, is one of the most common prayers spoken to Jesus in the New Testament: "Lord, have mercy."

Simple. Life giving.

The simplicity itself is part of the attraction. It aligns with the act of breathing. We can breathe in as we pray "Lord Jesus Christ, Son of God," and breathe out as we pray "have mercy on me, a sinner."

And of course, we all need mercy.

We need mercy for our weakness.

We need mercy for our woundedness.

We need mercy for our wickedness.

"Be still and know that I am God" (Psalm 46:10). Praying the Jesus prayer is a way to center, be still, and let God love me. When I am particularly anxious about life, I try to get away to somewhere quiet and pray this prayer.

Years ago, I was given a prayer rope (much like a rosary) from a hermitage in Berryville, Arizona. I wear it nearly all the time, often running my fingers and thumb over the rope, quietly saying the Jesus Prayer as my

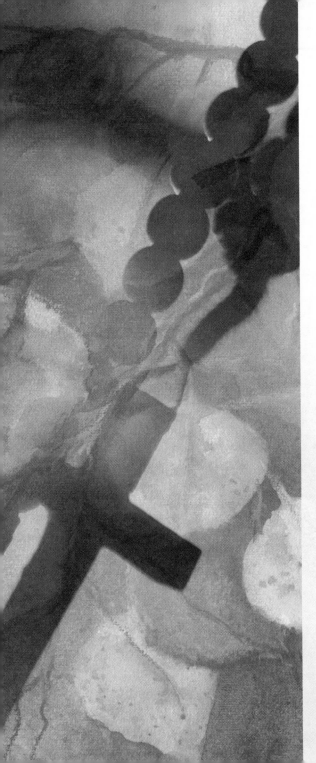

fingers touch each knot.

Just as athletes and musicians repeat exercises and scales in order for the skills to become second-nature, praying the Jesus Prayer has made it possible for me to live out Paul's perplexing call to "pray without ceasing" (1 Thessalonians 5:17). I can pray while doing tasks that do not require my full attention, such as walking or doing dishes. I have even come to pray it instinctively while sitting in traffic on I-25. It reminds me of the presence of God and that our Lord Jesus, indeed, has abundant mercy to give.

Although this spiritual practice is primarily for personal meditation, I pray the prayer for others as well—replacing the word "me" with the names of family, friends, and others. When I pray in this way I typically drop the last two words, "a sinner." It is enough for me to recognize the sin in *myself* as I pray.

The Jesus Prayer is a part of my work with clients at the Justice and Mercy Legal Aid Center. Going to court can be a daunting experience. Emotions run high. Difficult questions posed by attorneys or the judge can cause real anxiety for clients. Sometimes I prepare clients by sharing the Jesus Prayer and inviting them to pray when they are testifying, silently breathing the prayer in and out. I have seen it calm frayed nerves and prevent someone from stating anything other than the truth—always best when you are under oath, not to mention in any other life situation.

This prayer, and the awareness it brings to me moment by moment, is a gift for every season of life.

Lord Jesus Christ, Son of God, have mercy on me, a sinner.

—*Steve Thompson*

Sweet Relief for Homeless Families

Lining the sidewalk on Park Avenue, sleeping under the "Jesus Saves" neon light, flying a cardboard sign at the stoplight—the homeless people in full view might lead one to believe that homelessness primarily plagues single men. But the reality is that 39% of Colorado's total homeless population is comprised of families with children.[1]

Families who are homeless are less likely to live in shelters or sleep on the streets, making their challenges more invisible. And yet, the phone rings endlessly at Joshua Station—every day dozens of mothers and fathers are desperately seeking a safe home for their children.

Trunk-or-Treat

Motels are expensive, shelters can feel unsafe, supportive family members might have nothing more than a simple couch to offer—oftentimes homeless families are hustling to and from various locations, weekly or even nightly. None of these scenarios are stable or comfortable. None of these options are healthy for kids or their parents. None of these temporary solutions help families pursue self-sufficiency or fulfilment.

At Joshua Station, homeless families are given a place to call *home*. Walking into a room with beds, dressers, and even stuffed animals of their own is just the beginning of a deep sigh of relief.

Deep wounds and trauma are unavoidable for those who have experienced the instability and anxiety of homelessness. For us at Joshua Station, the housing we provide is merely the beginning. Real change comes through comprehensive and compassionate programs tailored to each family: everything from financial classes to children's play therapy, and from family advocacy to job coaching.

It is an intense process as families are welcomed into something special, something they are not accustomed to accepting or embracing. It is a process of

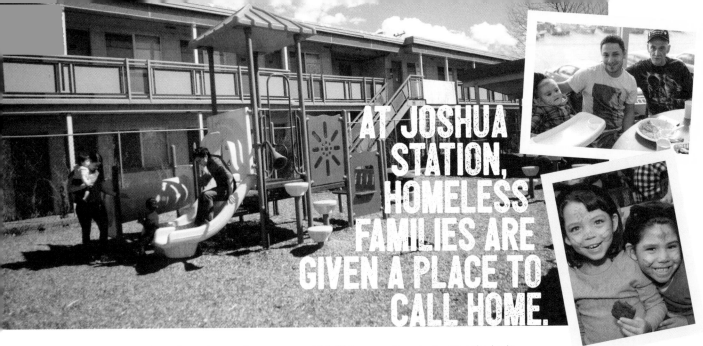

AT JOSHUA STATION, HOMELESS FAMILIES ARE GIVEN A PLACE TO CALL HOME.

transformation that allows for mothers, fathers, and grandparents to exhale and settle in.

Yet it's also true that all the programs and structure in the world don't make for *home*. Home is made up of the informal—yet intricate—experience of normalcy, ownership, and safety. In our old renovated motel, the proof is in the play. A game of tag with neighbors, laughter in the office hallways, a rowdy community dinner every Thursday night—all are signs of vibrant community life.

As autumn chills the air and frost kisses the earth, healing takes the shape of the annual Halloween Trunk-or-Treat.

Sam Trujillo, a former staff member and Denver native, imagined sharing part of his Chicano culture by inviting the Lady Low Riders to round up the coolest cars in town and host a fall carnival for past and current residents of Joshua Station. Now, ten years later, it is a beloved tradition on our little lot by the interstate highway.

Think of it! Dozens of shiny, tricked-out cars sporting spider webs and ghosts—all packed to the brim with candy.

Recovering from homelessness takes a lot of love and support from agencies like ours, *and* it also requires experiences of face-painting, roaring laughter, and neighborly love on a blacktop in the late October breeze.

—*Rebecca Mendoza Nunziato*

MAPPING THE HOPE OF A CITY

30 Years of Growth

Autumn invites us to pause in gratitude for the harvest. This doesn't come easily for helpers, missionaries, or other would-be agents of change. There is, after all, so much work to do. So much suffering. And so many living without an abiding awareness of how fully they are held within the loving hand of God.

Accepting Oscar Romero's invitation to "stop and take the long view," I find much for which to be grateful.

Thirty years ago, when Mile High Ministries was beginning, it was not common for churches to give much attention or resource in response to the poor. The idea that God has a special heart for the poor was not broadly embraced as central to Christian spirituality.

> IF I WERE TO MAP HOPE IN OUR CITY, I WOULD LOOK FOR PEOPLE SO TAKEN BY THE STORY OF GOD'S PRESENCE AMONG US **THAT THEY SPEND THEIR OWN LIVES BEING PRESENT, SHARING THEIR LIVES WITH OTHERS.**

For at least a century, Christianity in white America has been "lop-sided," with one wing of the church emphasizing a vertical expression of spirituality (personal relationship with God) and another emphasizing a horizontal dimension (glorifying God by making a better world). It's worth noting that the black church has long modeled a more holistic way of connecting spirituality and social concern.[1]

Around the time Frank Tillapaugh, a Denver pastor, wrote about "unleashing the church" for service in an urbanizing world, Ron Sider sounded an alarm about local and global poverty in his book "Rich Christians in an Age of Hunger."[2] During this era, John Perkins offered practical ways for some of those rich Christians to live in supportive solidarity with the poor.

The surprising thing was that all three of these thought-leaders, each of whom helped shape the DNA of Mile High Ministries, were evangelicals, writing from the center of that part of the church that had once focused solely on the vertical dimension of spirituality.

One can't deny that their voices made a difference. Today most churches I encounter make an effort to connect spirituality with some expression of compassion toward the poor.

I know: this is not to say that all is well in the church. Injustice and poverty remain. We can avoid the poor in our own neighborhood, even on our way to serve them overseas. Feel-good charity is still more common than strategic, dignity-focused compassion. Recent presidential elections have exposed deep divisions in the Christian community—divisions that many black and brown Christians were always able to see more clearly than those of us who are white.

But this is autumn, a season that invites us to pause and give thanks for what is ripe and abundant in the harvest: I'm grateful that the spirituality of today's church is a bit less "lop-sided" than it was a generation ago.

Today we could easily trace evidence of this hopeful trend across a map of Denver—a city filled with people whose abiding faith in God is expressed in love for their most vulnerable neighbors.

If I were to map hope in our city, I would look for people so taken by the story of God's presence among us that they spend their own lives being present, sharing their lives with others.

Network Coffee House, "God's living room" for the chronically homeless and mentally ill on Capitol Hill, is one place to find such people. So are the folks at **Dry Bones**, who look past the chaotic shell of homeless youth to see them as kids, and to connect with them at the level of the heart.

KIDS & TEENS

Speaking of kids, in just about any Denver neighborhood where kids face extra obstacles in life you're likely to find volunteers from **Save Our Youth** mentoring children; **Whiz Kids** tutors helping elementary students; **Colorado Uplift** teaching values and modeling virtues; and **Young Life** inviting kids to go to camp for the "best week of their lives." A map of hope in Denver would be filled with pins for these loving communities.

DENVER CHURCHES

There are too many good churches in our city to even know where to begin. Ask Pastor Jack at **New Life in Christ,** just off of west Colfax, about his congregation. He will likely pull out a photo album and tell you about one of his deacons who has such a servant heart for the community that you'd never guess he spent decades caught-up in drugs and violence. Ms. Eddie and Pastor Bob at **Agape Church** in Five Points have leveraged modest resources to provide enormous support for men and women coming out of prison. I'm always amazed by the big ministries coming from small neighborhood churches—it's like the miracle of fish-and-loaves replicated daily.

"Pure and faultless religion includes looking after orphans and widows in their distress." (James 1:27) At **Colorado Community Church**, pure and faultless religion looks like recruiting and training foster parents to open their homes and give their lives to kids in the system who have been waiting for a family.

AFFORDABLE HOUSING

Lack of affordable housing drives poverty and homelessness in the city. I'm grateful for passionate housing providers trying to keep up with the need. **The Colorado Village Collaborative** is trying a creative approach, building tiny-home villages with homeless people. And I'm inspired by an experiment at **Providence Bible Church** inviting homeowners to open up a few of the 150,000 extra bedrooms in our city that will be empty tonight for those who are taking steps toward self-sufficiency.

The crew at **Cross-Purpose** in northeast Denver are such thoughtful students of the city. They work hard to build effective pathways for people to escape poverty. This work of empowerment (helping people expand their own capacities) is more complex than just doing *for* others. It's why I'm grateful for **skilled business owners** like **Devin** who hires dozens of formerly-incarcerated men at his millwork company. Or **Helen**, who is leveraging a remarkable career in business to help under-served people build their own careers.

Immigrants are among our most vulnerable—and resilient— neighbors. **Casa de Paz** offers a place to stay and generous hospitality to families whose loved ones languish in immigration detention, as well as to people who have been recently released. I know that people reading these words have differing views on the politics of immigration, but doesn't this kind of hospitality seem like something Jesus would do?

When asked the most important thing for us to do, Jesus said; "Love God and love your neighbor." Local Denver leaders **Dave and Jay** have helped ignite a national movement to remember what it means to love our actual neighbors—the people who live near us. **Greg and Karen** embody it with an annual East Side picnic with their neighbors, many of whom are gang members—a tradition that began when a neighbor was killed in a drive-by shooting at the end of Greg and Karen's block: death giving birth to new life.

That East Side picnic began as an effort for one person to help another but has endured as a celebratory experience of kinship and mutual transformation. Unlikely friendships are helping realize, in the words of novelist Luis Alberto Urrea, "there is no us and them; there is only us."[4]

INTERFAITH

Although my own network is mostly within Christian circles, the "us" certainly includes those of other faiths. One of my friends and partners is **Imam Ali** at the Northeast Denver Islamic Center, whose care for the poor is leading them to build affordable housing in a gentrifying neighborhood.

WE'VE BARELY BEGUN TO MAP THE HOPE OF OUR CITY. THESE PLACES DO AS MUCH TO MAKE DENVER LOVELY AS DO OUR MOUNTAINS OR OUR 300 DAYS OF SUNSHINE. AND, WE DIDN'T MENTION THE TEACHERS, CIVIL SERVANTS, MEDICAL WORKERS, EMERGENCY RESPONDERS, POLITICIANS, ACTIVISTS, ADVOCATES, AND JUST REGULAR FOLKS WHO ARE, EACH IN THEIR OWN WAY, ON EVERY BLOCK AND IN EVERY SCHOOL, BRINGING PEOPLE TOGETHER, PUSHING BACK AGAINST THE DARKNESS, REFUSING TO LET DESPAIR HAVE THE LAST WORD.

I WONDER WHAT PEOPLE AND PLACES YOU WOULD ADD?

—*Jeff Johnsen*

NORTH SIDE HIGHLANDS

A Tale of Two Neighborhoods

Come spend an afternoon in two of the most interesting neighborhoods in our city. One has been the emotional heart of Denver's Chicano community for generations. The other has become one of the hippest neighborhoods in the city for a younger, more affluent, mostly white group of residents.

You won't have to travel far to visit both places. Because, they are the very same neighborhood.

What's in a Name?

While newcomers might call the area Highlands, or use the name of one of the other smaller neighborhoods in this part of the city, long-time neighbors simply call it the *North Side*. North Denver is bordered by Colfax on the south, 52nd Avenue on the north, I-25 on the east, and Sheridan Blvd on the west. The heart of the North Side runs east from Federal Boulevard, to the north of North High School.

In one way, the name Highland is much older. According to local historian Phil Goodstein, when "General" William Larimer jumped the claim on land that he was to name Denver City during the gold rush in 1859, he also laid claim to a parcel uphill to the northwest. He then laid out a town called Highland as an "insurance policy" in case things didn't pan out in Denver—no pun intended. Not much came of Highland, or of the streetcar suburb Highlands to its west, and the names faded from memory.[1]

In recent years variations on those old names—Highland, West Highland, LoHi, and others—have been given, formally or informally, to neighborhoods in the heart of the North Side. For many North Siders, calling the old neighborhood something else feels like a thinly-disguised way of erasing their presence to make way for something new, and more importantly for *someone* new.

Reflective questions: *Does your neighborhood have a name? Who chose it? How does it help define your community?*

Mapping Hope and Pain

Wherever humans live, we create stories of hope and pain. One way to know a neighborhood is to map places that represent some of those stories. Here are just a few North Side examples...

■ **North High School** at 2960 Speer Blvd has been the visual and emotional center of the North Side for decades. The neighborhood takes great pride in North High. The drama of Denver Public Schools has played out here in very public ways, as well, as neighbors

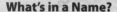
North High School

HIGHLAND
NORTH SIDE

52nd AVE
I-25
I-70
SHERIDAN BLVD
COLFAX AVE
FEDERAL BLVD
I-25
6th AVE
ALAMEDA

have fought for their school in the face of declining enrollment and a series of turnarounds and reinventions.

■ For decades **Escuela Tlatelolco**, led by family members of civil rights pioneer Corky Gonzalez, provided both alternative education and a sense of community pride for young Chicanos across the street from North High at 2949 Federal Boulevard.

■ **The State Home for Dependent and Neglected Children** was built in 1895 at 3233 Vallejo Street. Just the name conjures the deep sadness in which so many kids lived their early lives.

■ **Columbus Park / La Raza Park** on 38th Avenue between Navajo and Osage is officially named in recognition of the Italian-American community that dominated the neighborhood once known as Little Italy. By the 1960s Denver's Chicano community began calling it La Raza Park. Long time North Siders have memories of family outings and political rallies in the park. And also of violent clashes with the police during some of those rallies.

■ The history of Denver's North Side inevitably includes stories about **mafia-related violence**, like the 1933 death of "kingpin" Joe Roma who was gunned down in his living room on Vallejo Street while practicing the mandolin. Decades later numerous young North Siders lost their lives to other expressions of gang violence. For some reason, mafia violence has come to acquire an almost romantic fascination

Saint Patrick's Catholic Church

Our Lady of Mount Carmel Catholic Church

The Parish-Shrine of Our Lady of Guadalupe

for our culture. Yet each violent death is an incalculable tragedy for a family and community.

Faith on the North Side

Perhaps more than most Denver neighborhoods, you can learn much about the North Side by paying attention to its many churches. Here is a small sample, all within walking distance of one another:

■ **Saint Patrick's Catholic Church** (33rd and Pecos) was once the center of Denver's Irish Community. Today, a monastery occupies most of the block. The "Poor Clares," an order of Franciscan Capuchin, women live a cloistered, contemplative life— "a visible sign of our total consecration to God."[2]

■ "Mother" Frances Cabrini, known as the Patron Saint of Immigrants and an advocate for the poor, helped Italian immigrants plant **Our Lady of Mount Carmel Catholic Church** (36th and Navajo) in the 1890s.

■ The church at 36th and Kalamath is officially **The Parish-Shrine of Our Lady of Guadalupe**. Though it feels like a quiet retreat tucked into the lee of the interstate, three thousand people gather for worship here every week. For decades it was a catalyst of social justice activism.

- **Highlands Community Church** meets in the historic Holiday Theatre at 2644 W. 32nd Avenue and was one of Denver's first churches from the evangelical tradition to fully embrace LGBTQ people.
- **Our Merciful Savior Church** (32nd and Wyandot) once served Welsh and Cornish miners and has long had a reputation as a modest congregation with a robust outreach to the poor, especially immigrants.

Reflective question: *How do you imagine the role of ethnically homogeneous churches might be similar or different from a century ago? If you are part of a faith community, how do you think it will be remembered by its neighborhood in a generation or two?*

Vanishing Healer

Over several weeks in the fall of 1895 perhaps one hundred thousand people stood in line around the modest bungalow at 3225 Quivas Street for the chance to have 39-year-old immigrant cobbler Francis Schlatter lay his hands on them and quietly pray for their healing. Schlatter gave no sermons and would accept no money. Many thousands claimed to be healed. Then suddenly, he slipped out of town and never returned.

Reflective Questions: *What is your impression upon hearing a story like this one? A miracle, a swindle, or something else? What would it take to convince you otherwise?*

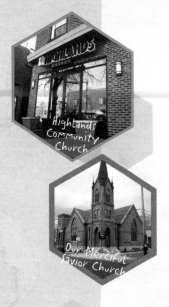

Neighborhoods Change—But This Time Feels Different

On the old North Side, Mexican immigrants lived with Chicanos in a community that had once been Italian, and before that Irish. Latinos had moved into the North Side just as Italians were leaving for the "good life" in larger suburban homes. The "disinvestment" caused by one community moving out had created an opportunity for the next group.

The sudden influx of people and money reshaping today's North Side feels different than past demographic shifts. This time a more prosperous group—mostly progressive white people who, ironically, value diversity and even moved to the city hoping to live among a mixed population—is rapidly displacing communities of color who might have wished to stay. The whole process seems not only "too big to fail," but too big to even question.

Today the Highlands are buzzing with boutiques and restaurants and specialty shops—super cool places with descriptions like "apothecary"

or "ramen enclave." The remodeled homes are lovely. The landscaping is fabulous. There are signs of genuine community: street festivals, dog socialization events, outdoor yoga classes. There is so much goodness to appreciate. You'll see all the signs of this newness as you walk the neighborhood.

Perhaps you'll see the vanishing signs of the old North Side as well, and of long-time residents who wonder where they will fit, if they can afford to stay at all.

My friend's grandparents owned a house on the North Side for decades and were thrilled to sell it in 2012 for over $250,000. The new owner sold it a month later for $370,000. Six months later it sold for more than $600,000, and three years later for almost $900,000.

Reflective Questions: *What is your impression upon hearing a story like this one? A miracle, a swindle, or something else? What would it take to convince you otherwise?*

Can you identify a time when a well-intentioned group brought unwelcome change into your life? How about the other side of the coin: have you been the person bringing or representing unwelcome change?

Pursuing a Deeper Reality… and a Good Meal

Share your impressions from the day over a meal at a North Side institution like Pizza Alley on 32nd Avenue or the Original Chubby's on 38th.

End your North Side pilgrimage with the Prayer for Our City found on page 251 of this book;

"Help us see this place as something other than a battleground between us and them, where our imaginations are limited by win/lose propositions and endless rivalry. Show us a deeper reality, God: a place where former rivals and natural enemies work and play together in peace, and where all people enjoy communion with you."

—Jeff Johnsen

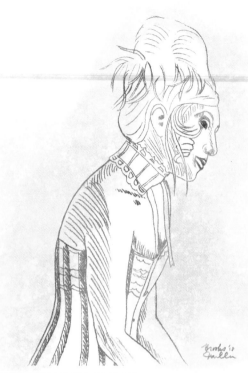

LIZZIE
PRESTON

Lizzie Preston and Vincent Harding

Inconvenient Heroes

izzie Preston might seem an unlikely choice for autumn "Denver Street Saint." She leveraged what most would consider an unholy life into an opportunity to lead—and lead heroically.

The background to her story was a divisive and ugly political climate. The presidential race of 1880 was very close, with Democrats and Republicans exploiting resentment against Chinese immigrants to gain votes. Because Colorado was a new state, its small electoral vote could help swing the election. Hundreds of people from other states rode the rails to Denver, intending only to vote and leave.

In Colorado, the Chinese population had become the scapegoats for tension between miners and mine owners over wages and working conditions. Local labor leader Stephen Vinot printed racist screeds from his office at the corner of 13th Avenue and Lipan Street, blaming Chinese immigrants for unemployment, crime, and even for corrupting American morals.

Sunday afternoon before the election, at a bar called John's Place at 16th Street and Wazee, three white men picked a fight with two Chinese men who had been playing billiards. Rumors spilled onto the streets that a gang of Chinese had attacked and even shot innocent people.

Though there is no proof, it seems as if the entire incident had been planned in advance, because in a matter of minutes a crowd of 3,000 people—mostly men—gathered in front of the American House and Hotel at 16th and Blake chanting "Death to Chinese."

Mayor Sopris ordered Denver's fire department to use a fire hose on the crowd as it moved up 16th Street, hoping to get them wet and cold enough to go home. This only enraged the drunken mob, which swarmed up Halladay (now named Market) Street, attacking Chinese men and cutting off their queues—the long braids worn by nearly all Chinese men.

One of those Chinese men was twenty-eight-year-old Look Young who worked in the Sing Lee Laundry at 19th and Lawrence, and who sent his wages home to support his wife and parents in a village near Canton. The mob smashed its way into the Sing Lee Laundry, seized Look Young and dragged him down Arapahoe Street to 18th Street, with dozens of men taking a turn to hit or kick Look Young. Eventually two older white women and a medical doctor finally pulled his broken body from the ravenous mob. It was too late: he was dead. As though sated by the blood of the innocent scapegoat, the mob began to dissipate.

Chinese homes and businesses were clustered around Denver's red-light district (from which Market Street derives its name). As the sun began to set, local madam Lizzie Preston led a group of white female prostitutes out onto Market Street. They ran ahead of the violent crowd, physically surrounding Chinese people to form a human shield and escort them to the county jail at 14th and Arapaho. There, 200 Chinese were sheltered for their own protection. It was a courageous act of leadership and love for

LIZZIE PRESTON LEVERAGED WHAT MOST WOULD CONSIDER AN UNHOLY LIFE INTO AN OPPORTUNITY TO LEAD—AND LEAD HEROICALLY.

these women to put their own bodies between a bloodthirsty mob and its victims—bodies whose dignity or safety was of little regard to most of the men rampaging through the streets of Denver.

Over the next few days, Denver's Chinese feared more violence in the wake of the election which would inevitably be a bitter loss to one side or the other. They had nothing left to tether them to Denver: every Chinese business in the city and most of their private homes had been destroyed; they had no money for leaving town to somewhere safer, or even to buy food.

Lizzie Preston convinced the Union Pacific to give half price fares to Chinese who wished to leave town. She put up $200 (nearly $5,000 in 2018) of her own money and raised another $1,050 from local madams to buy train tickets for their Chinese neighbors. Lizzie and her "girls"

VINCENT HARDING

made baskets of cooked food for the journey, walked the Chinese to Union Station and waited with them until they were safely on the train.

No reparations were ever paid to Denver's Chinese. Numerous rioters paid small fines to the city. The men who killed Look Young were acquitted of murder, merely serving short sentences for rioting.

Two years later, with leadership from Colorado's own Senator Teller, the U.S. Congress passed the country's first-ever immigration law: the Chinese Exclusion Act, which was not fully overturned until 1965.

Nearly a century later, Vincent Harding wrote an important book about another "inconvenient hero," his friend and fellow civil rights activist Dr. Martin Luther King, Jr.

Vincent would have liked Lizzie's spunk, and the way she risked body and fortune to stand in solidarity with vulnerable people.

In fact, he seemed to genuinely like... everyone. A lifetime of struggle for justice can make activists bitter or cynical. Not so with Vincent, whose spirituality seemed to connect him to a fountain of lovingkindness and inclusion.

Born and raised in New York City, Dr. Harding came to Denver from teaching and leadership roles throughout the country to teach at the Iliff School of Theology. Once in Denver, he also curated the Veterans of Hope Project, collecting the wisdom of veterans of social-change movements. In the 1960's, he and his wife Rosemarie had participated in some of the critical moments of the Civil Rights Movement. Together they co-founded an interracial service center called Mennonite House in Atlanta, Georgia, which was one model when Mile High Ministries opened the Issachar Community (today called the Issachar Center for Urban Leadership) in 1998.

As a scholar and writer, Vincent was called upon to compose speeches for Dr. King—so closely connected were their convictions and actions. Some of those convictions were broadly unpopular: perhaps the most consequential speech that Vincent wrote for Dr. King was delivered at Riverside Church in New York City exactly one year before King's assassination. In that speech, "A Time to Break Silence," King broke with the Johnson administration over the Vietnam War, thereby losing a powerful friend in the White House and making himself unpopular with many people of all races.

Though we have come to think of Dr. King as a nearly universally-inspiring American hero, his friend Dr. Harding argued he was more radical in his views on eradicating war and poverty—views firmly rooted in his prophetic brand of Christianity—than many wish to remember.

Dr. Harding was himself a prophetic voice who could speak challenging truth, yet love always came through. He acted upon his convictions with gentle openness and patience. He built relationships that crossed boundaries of culture, worldview and generation—such relationships were critical for the movement to go beyond politics in the direction of equity and a "beloved community" in which former rivals and natural enemies

could work together in peace.

In a reflection on the life of German theologian and protest martyr Dietrich Bonhoeffer, Vincent Harding wrote, "Teach us how to love

"TEACH US HOW TO LOVE AMERICA AND ITS PEOPLE SO MUCH THAT WE WILL RISK OUR LIVES IN THE STRUGGLE FOR TRANSFORMATION, FOR THE NEW CITY, FOR THE NEW LAND."

America and its people so much that we will risk our lives in the struggle for transformation, for the new city, for the new land."

Jesus said, "Blessed are those who hunger and thirst for righteousness and justice." Blessed are you, Lizzie Preston and Vincent Harding. Thank you for sacrificing and for taking risks. Thank you for acting forcefully and lovingly in the face of ignorance and hatred, on behalf of those whom God loves. Your prophetic voice will continue to ring in our city.

—*Jeff Johnsen*

November

LANGAR

A Meal for Equality and Oneness

Barren trees surround Civic Center Park as fall transitions to winter. On any given day one might see churches or nonprofits stationed to hand out brown bag lunches to the homeless. If you've ever participated, you know the standard fare: a simple sandwich, a granola bar, and an apple. The line forms, and the shuffle begins. But on one particular November day a very unique meal is served: a smorgasbord of noodles, chutneys, samosas, and other vegetarian treats—all creating a traditional meal of the Sikh religion called *Langar*. This meal, served to the hungry and homeless, is a custom for Sikh communities across the world. As a result, over 6.5 million Langar meals are served each day! Here in Denver, beautiful and unlikely partnerships have formed alongside the Colorado Sikhs: evangelicals working with Muslims; the Church of Religious Science working with Methodists; Buddhists working with various non-profits—all joined together to realize a shared goal of caring for the poor.

Langar's centuries-old purpose of promoting the "equality and oneness of all humankind" is accomplished in Denver not only through the sharing of food each November, but also through the boundary-crossing partnerships it inspires. Langar is an example of *the prophetic imagination*, a phrase introduced by theologian Walter Brueggemann.[1] It is the telling of an alternative story, the practicing of hope while facing pain, and the expression of God's heart for those who are oppressed. What better holy day than one in which the breaking of bread is celebrated with friends, former enemies, and the marginalized?

—*Rebecca Mendoza Nunziato*

Stirring the Sauce

Jazmin's Journey

Jazmin[1] is writing a book. She tells me it's her "book of special sauce."

Since I know Jazmin to be an extraordinary woman with a fascinating life, I'm excited to hear of her project. When I tell her I'll be eager to read her book, she pauses. It seems I'm not her target audience.

It's a children's book, she explains—for her own two children, Natalia and Joaquin. It is not a book of parental advice, she stresses, but rather of experiential wisdom. She wants her children to know the essential ingredients of who they are, individually and as a family. The water. The picante and the dulce. The fire, the stirring, and the fermentation. All these are ingredients in her family's special sauce.

Jazmin says that she got this idea of a special sauce from Mile High Ministries, and especially by serving on the board of directors for the past seven years. "That's how Jeff Johnsen talks about what is essential to our organizational identity. "Our board is a lot more than just financial decision-makers; we help the organization become more true to itself by tending to that special sauce, even if it is harder to put into words than a mission statement. The special sauce comes from stories, and we are part of the actual stories that make the sauce."

Jazmin has lived the stories of this organization and faith community in more ways than most: as a teen mentee of our community partners, a college-age apprentice at our Issachar Center for Urban Leadership, a client at our Justice and Mercy Legal Aid Center, a contractor, a donor, a mentor herself, and eventually as a board member entrusted with fiduciary responsibility and visionary leadership for our 501(c)3 nonprofit corporation.

"I'm amazed, really, when I think about how I've grown through these roles—and how my life has been woven through them. My life is so full now as a mom, and I wear many hats in our home. One way I think about being a mom is that, together with my husband, I am executive director of my family. What is our identity and mission? How do we take that seriously? What has come before us that makes us who we are, and where are we going? What are our challenges and strategies? How is God leading, and what should our own spiritual leadership look like?"

JAZMIN HAS LIVED THE STORIES OF THIS ORGANIZATION AND FAITH COMMUNITY IN MORE WAYS THAN MOST: AS A TEEN MENTEE OF OUR COMMUNITY PARTNERS, A COLLEGE-AGE APPRENTICE AT OUR ISSACHAR CENTER FOR URBAN LEADERSHIP, A CLIENT AT OUR JUSTICE AND MERCY LEGAL AID CENTER, A CONTRACTOR, A DONOR, A MENTOR HERSELF, AND EVENTUALLY AS A BOARD MEMBER ENTRUSTED WITH FIDUCIARY RESPONSIBILITY AND VISIONARY LEADERSHIP

Jazmin grew up strong and independent, in a city a world away from Denver. Abandoned by her father at age four and her mother at age eleven, she was crisscrossing Mexico City by herself by age twelve. Her grandmother and godmother were major influences and caregivers, but Jazmin was rebellious and angry. She channeled her aggression through Taekwondo. Energetic and gifted, she excelled academically. The capital city itself was Jazmin's home and the stage for her dreams—she knew it and was in love with it.

One day when Jazmin was thirteen, there was a knock at the front door where she was staying with her aunt. It was her mother, demanding that Jazmin come with her. Over her aunt's strenuous objections, Jazmin complied. Four days later, Jazmin was in a Juarez hotel she can only describe as "very sketchy." There was a car. A river. A bridge. Two crossings. Jazmin was captured, incarcerated, and separated from her mother. She cried herself to sleep, and later woke up in a room with only a blanket. There was an American official, a bribe, and a "coyote" to take her further—she didn't know where. She was dropped off in the middle of the night in an El Paso trailer park with a man she had never met—scared and defenseless. There was the drive to Denver, a city she had never heard of.

JAZMIN WAS ACCEPTED INTO A TWO-YEAR RESIDENTIAL APPRENTICESHIP IN ISSACHAR CENTER'S LEADERSHIP DEVELOPMENT PROGRAM

With bewildering suddenness, Jazmin found herself in the hallways of West High School. English was foreign, along with most everything else.

Soon Jazmin met Trudy Swain, vice president of our partner organization Save Our Youth. Trudy became her mentor, as did Maureen Lord. Maureen, who Jazmin calls her "angel," patiently taught Jazmin English—over rounds of golf! And patiently shared her own ways of everyday connection with God, which shape Jazmin profoundly to this day. For a month each summer, Jazmin lived with Maureen and soaked up new experiences. Maureen's advocacy and Jazmin's tenacity opened doors, including acceptance into several Colorado universities. Lacking funding for schools such as CU Boulder and UNC Greely, Jazmin enrolled at Metro State in Denver.

At the same time, Jazmin was also accepted into a two-year residential apprenticeship in Issachar Center's leadership development program, which for her would grow into a life-long experience of family. It was a deep dive from the start! One of the very first things Jazmin experienced was a walk through one of the most distressed city blocks in all of Denver, on the northeast side. Low, tiny brick residences crumbled among overgrown weeds—by all appearances, abandoned.

"We picked our way through broken glass and syringes and found places to sit on broken-off tree branches as Jeff told us the story of the place, which had once been a nice community. The devastation we saw was primarily the work of one notorious slumlord who lived somewhere else. When Jeff told us there were still people staying on the block, I couldn't believe it. It must have been worse than camping, and a lot more dangerous. I was shocked that this guy could get away with it for all these years."

As the Issachar apprentices explored the blighted property, Jazmin suddenly blurted out, "I can imagine this as a great place to live someday!" Today she remembers that moment as a first step in her journey of learning what it means to not only have vision, but how to put that vision into

JAZMIN EXPERIENCED WAS A WALK THROUGH ONE OF THE MOST DISTRESSED CITY BLOCKS IN ALL OF DENVER... JAZMIN SUDDENLY BLURTED OUT, "I CAN IMAGINE THIS AS A GREAT PLACE TO LIVE SOMEDAY!"

practical action. Years later she is on the board of directors, working to implement that very vision on that very city block—as a redevelopment project called Clara Brown Commons. "We own the vision with Jeff and share accountability for what's needed to make it happen. There are a lot of obstacles and it's truly a journey of faith in God. I see it as a chance to pour more of the special sauce into a community!"

The sauce has been poured into Jazmin's own family. On a Saturday

JONATHAN WAS ALSO AN APPRENTICE AT ISSACHAR AND THEIR TIME AT ISSACHAR OVERLAPPED, PROVIDING RICH COMMUNITY LIFE FOR THEIR GROWTH AS A COUPLE. "WE CONTINUE TO LEAN ON FRIENDS TO HOLD US ACCOUNTABLE TO OUR FAMILY'S SPECIAL SAUCE.

evening in 2006 at Westside Christian Fellowship in Denver, Jazmin was married to her husband Jonathan—with Jeff Johnsen officiating. The long walk to this moment of beauty was not without stumbles and hard turns. They had fallen in love in high school, despite warnings from concerned friends that Jonathan was "a bad person." Eventually sensing they might

be right, Jazmin broke off the relationship. When they ran into each other later at Save Our Youth, Jazmin says, "God said to me, 'he's the one.' I can't explain how I heard that, because I didn't have any idea of how God speaks. I had no proof that Jonathan had changed in any way. But I soon found out that he had, in big ways." Jonathan was also an apprentice at Issachar and their time at Issachar overlapped, providing rich community life for their growth as a couple. "We continue to lean on friends to hold us accountable to our family's special sauce."

I ask Jazmin to share secrets of the recipe. "**Sankofa**," she begins—from the Twi language of Ghana meaning *go back and get it.* "For Issachar apprentices, it means to never forget our roots. They will always have something to teach us." Jazmin knows well the pain of having no secure home, "living everywhere and nowhere." She knows betrayal, rejection, and sorrow. Memories sting, and current realities can overwhelm. "I know that life in God is not always pretty. I think of the life of Jesus on earth, how he experienced all these hardships."

"**Compassion**," Jazmin continues. "To be vulnerable with others, to feel what they are going through, and to expose ourselves to the world's pain. So many people around us live in poverty. I know that God is compassionate, and we have the opportunity to show our compassion." Jazmin explains that this part of her family's mission requires trust, not only trust in God but trust in the gifts of the struggling person—that they can be empowered. "I love rallying other moms to be all they can be. I love being at Joshua Station, sharing family times with our kids together on the playground there. I love to give, and I love to be grateful."

"**Faith**" sustains Jazmin every day. "God has brought me a long, long way," she says. "It's so crazy out there, especially these days, and especially for people in society who come from where I do. But I also think of promised land, of God saying 'I got you.'"

We're just getting going with ingredients. "Oh other things, too, for instance…." But instead of a bullet point, she begins another story that will leave both of us with moist eyes. The sauce has been stirred and simmered, and isn't finished yet.

—*Scott Dewey*

"The world, this palpable world, which we were wont to treat with the boredom and disrespect with which we habitually regard places with no sacred association for us, is in truth a holy place, and we did not know it. Venite, adoremus."[1]

—Teilhard de Chardin

Liberation Ecology

Waking Up to Oneness

Breath.
Creation flows from the mouth of the Creator.
Let there be.
Let there be.

Silence.
World warming in unison, life bursts into existence.
An existence impossible without love.
An existence manifest, breath by beloved breath.

Light.
Particles scattering across the universe.
Waves of welcome refracting into mystical spectrum.
"Invincibly one in endless diversity."

Gravity.
Dance of duality—holding everything together.
It has always been there.
In the dust of galaxies, in the eternal gaze of God,
Christ.

—Rebecca Mendoza Nunziato

My eyes welled up when I heard the words: *All things are unexplainably, invincibly one in endless diversity forever.*[2]

It spoke to something deep within me—something our ancestors have always known, something caught in glimpses and whispers.

Yet we forget. Children know these things, but along the way we grow up and grow away from what we used to know.

To wander among the trees, to let the wind dance across bare skin, sink toes into the cold earth is to remember. To breathe in the scent of rainfall is a kind of coming home.

What we remember is who we really are. So much more than mere rejuvenation, we are participating in salvation, becoming more fully human. We remember: We are all one.

Welcome to liberation, a rebirth. You'll see… **everything is holy.**

The Aztec Danza is one of the wisdom traditions that still survives today to remind us. Our First Nations brothers and sisters call us into the sacred rhythm of love through the beat of the drum.

Shells clacking at the ankles. A precious bark that burns and purifies the air. Feather headdresses waving in worship.

Communally, we turn directionally as the drum echoes in our hidden corner of the city.

To the East. *Tlapallan.*

To the North. *Mictlampa.*

To the West. *Cihuatlampa.*

To the South. *Huitzlampa.*

Then we honor the sky, hands raised.

The Earth. The danzante kneels, nearly kissing the earth. *I want to kiss the earth too.*

The center of our holy circle. We see each other and hold the space as sacred. *I wish I could dance like that.*

These seven directions ground us in place.

The drum, the heartbeat, reverberates through our bodies, the bodies we sometimes forget to love.

Carlos, the leader of the danzantes, turns and points to the 8th Avenue bridge: "I used to sleep under there." Going further back, his people lived here before the bridge, before society changed the rules of survival.

There, under the overpass—**everything is holy.**

My husband and I were reminded along a frosty trail one Sunday. Alone with that pure white blanket of snow, and a twinge of avalanche fear. Back at the trailhead we commented, "Isn't it strange we haven't seen any wildlife?" Then we stopped to listen.

The forest was alive. Buzzing just beyond sight. Birds chirping, and squirrels foraging the offerings of early Spring.

We had forgotten how to pay attention.

Go to the forest.

Everything is holy here.

✳ ✳ ✳

 lean over the balcony six floors up in a Capitol Hill apartment building: precious pedestrians and a flurry of cars. Some blast music, others laugh. Our city isn't quiet. We take our coffee beans roasted lightly and poured into cardboard or plastic. "To go, please."

I contemplate my fellow humans: all the Uber drivers, bike riders, and dog walkers on this block are beautiful. They are absolutely stunning in their grunge, glam, and Birkenstocks.

The bell chimes and my meditation is complete.

Go to the city.

Everything is holy here.

✳ ✳ ✳

t Mile High Ministries' offices, we commune at the industrial edge of the city. The South Platte River, not far from our backdoor, is lost in the sound and smells of the highway. Yet even here we are reminded, with monarch butterflies and the buzzing of bees around Autumn Joy bushes.

Our chapel sits in the middle of an alleyway easement. Tires, trash, and scattered glass decorate the edging. But we gather here, praying with "eyes wide open" to connect our urban hearts and minds to the life of God flowing through the birds and the tossed-aside beer cans, alike.

Both volunteers and residents participate in the liberation of this lot of land, caressing the urban jungle with a trash bag or spade in hand—**witnesses to the holy.**

✳ ✳ ✳

ot far from the most polluted zip code in America lies a city block ravaged by indifference and disrespect. What does resurrection mean to this forlorn place, where the stench of sadness lingers, where loss of life stains the concrete?

The soil weeps. Decades of damnation.

What of the cracked dirt? The twisted vines and worn-down grasses?

I wonder, what of this is holy?

Yet, a seed of holiness is lying dormant and expectant in the earth—a dream of what this block could become. A prayer for liberation. Redemption for the poor and those in desperate need of afford-able housing.

My home on wheels, a small RV with every-thing we need, is a place of liberation—from consumption, discontentment, and comparison with others. Instead, we celebrate just enough water, meager space for human possessions, and lots of bumping into one another in the kitchen.

In 200-square-feet we practice viewing all resources as precious; we embody solidarity with those who have no choice in this matter. We park on friends' property, learning to be better neighbors over community meals, weeding the garden, and sharing the patio.

We are unable to ignore the sacred seasonal shifts—fall comes straight through the walls and beckons us to pause and prepare; winter is close. **Each season—holy**.

Today's world—with its anxieties and chaos—cries out for us to come home. To bear witness.

To awaken to the breath of God in every living thing.

In fall we are acutely aware of the harvest; we gather to give thanks around a banquet table and begin to plan holiday giving. Our ancestors—and my people still today—move through the fields, nimble hands feeling the Earth produce.

How can we honor the holiness of this season? It is a sacrifice to love our planet and our neighbors, but this work is the work of liberation, of bearing witness to oneness.

Slow down. Bike, ride RTD, or walk as an act of worship.[3]

Eat with respect. less milk, less meat; more sea-sonal, more local. Compost food scraps. Next spring your garden will flourish in gratitude.

Ban bottled water. Bring your own coffee mug. Skip the straw.

As is often true of our spiritual practices, these actions seem small. We let our compassion spill out in hope that we are protecting the people and places we love. All are disciplines that we worry may never result in large-scale change. Yet life is a com-mitment to a way of being, a form of peacemaking and shalom-seeking, a faith in "a future not our own."

May we extend our celebration of oneness into concrete action for the good of this precious home we inhabit. May we find ourselves more and more connected with the heartbeat of this beautiful, unlikely planet.

—*Rebecca Mendoza Nunziato*

LET OUR COMPASSION SPILL OUT IN HOPE THAT WE ARE PROTECTING THE PEOPLE AND PLACES WE LOVE

A Final Blessing for Your Journey

May God Bless You with Discomfort

This blessing comes from a Benedictine Sister, Ruth Fox. Printed versions are displayed around our office. Sister Ruth's poetic prayer captures tensions that we have experienced during our thirty-year journey—heart break, frustration, relationship, celebration, peace, and hope for God's vision to be realized.

We offer this as the final benediction of our book and pray that you will be blessed in each of these ways:

May God bless you with discontent with easy answers, half-truths, superficial relationships, so that you will live from deep within your heart.

—〰〰—

May God bless you with anger at injustice, oppression, abuse, and exploitation of people, so that you will work for justice, equality, and peace.

—〰〰—

May God bless you with tears to shed for those who suffer from pain, rejection, starvation, and war, so that you will reach out your hand to comfort them and to change their pain to joy.

—〰〰—

May God bless you with the foolishness to think you can make a difference in this world, so that you will do the things which others tell you cannot be done.

—〰〰—

If you have the courage to accept these blessings, then God will also bless you with:

> *happiness*—because you will know that you have made life better for others
>
> *inner peace*—because you will have worked to secure peace for others
>
> *laughter*—because your heart will be light
>
> *faithful friends*—because you will accept your worth as persons

—〰〰—

These blessings are yours—not for the asking, but for the giving—from One who wants to be your companion, our God, who lives and reigns, forever and ever. Amen.

—*Sister Ruth Fox, OSB*

Healing is impossible in loneliness; it is the opposite of loneliness.

Conviviality is healing. To be healed we must come with all the other creatures to the feast of Creation." *— Wendell Berry. The Art of the Commonplace: The Agrarian Essays*

BEYOND OUR EFFORTS:

Christ

> *"We are prophets of a future not our own."*
> —Prayer of Oscar Romero

This is a statement of faith: Everything is becoming.

Every thing. Things stir within things, unsettled; whirls among whirls. Worlds. Particles and waves ripple across fields within atoms and solar systems, undulating like breeze-blown prairie grass.

Within the warm womb my cells divide. I'm smaller than a poppy seed, and no smarter. I sprout a brain stem, and in due course I flower forth a prefrontal cortex. My how time flies! In 13 short years I'm smarter than my parents. Space-time bends, life turns, and within a half century I'm inclining my ear and heart to their wisdom—which I'm bemused to discover consists mostly of inclining the ear and heart.

My city booms. Between busts, we burst with construction cranes and drilling rigs. We build up and tear down. We divide: we legislate and protest, we win and lose. We unite: we're of one accord most often in back yards and front stoops—but happily also in our city parks and cultural centers. We are becoming.

A statement of faith I say, that we actually are becoming. I climb out on an even longer limb to trust that we are part of ever-unfolding *goodness.* While human development, social upheaval, and galaxy expansion provide observable data points, the data sure is mixed. We walk by faith rather than sight when it comes to narrating meaning to it all. What in the world is going on? What if anything—amid quantum uncertainty, genetic determinism, a morning kiss, and the morning news—are we moving from, and moving toward?

Catch me on a sick-of-the-world day, and you might get one answer off the top of my head. On a happy-with-friends day, you might get another. But deep in my heart, "Oh deep in my heart," as the civil rights anthem has it, I do believe: We shall overcome. We'll walk hand in hand. We shall live in peace. I do believe that the present is poised, and the future is more beautiful than all of the pasts it enfolds and transcends.

We walk by faith rather than sight when it comes to narrating meaning to it all. What in the world is going on?

Suffice to say I haven't come by such faith easily, or maintained it without great heart-aching struggle. I don't know how anyone could. Someone has called it the audacity of hope. Someone has called it the pearl of great price.

I will call it Christ.

Christ is all. Everything that is becoming, *is becoming in Christ.*

Did you see that coming, as you began to read this? I haven't usually seen it coming either. Beneath the surface of things the divine current flows incognito, often unrecognized and unnamed. It has no need for us to name it, any more than fire needs a name in order to burn.

But we creatures of the prefrontal cortex need what stones and stars do not: language, and names, and faces to love. We may employ language for abstractions, with analytical precision satisfying to the mind. But we cannot eat an abstraction for breakfast, let alone give our hearts to one. We—yes we of the neurotransmitters and endorphins—need lyrics for the great inner stirrings. We name what we love, with many names, as I do with my beloved.

So I join with others in naming the becoming-of-all-things *Christ*. Christ, into whose lovingkindness I was born. Christ, to whom I am in the life-long process of giving myself. Christ to whom every thing is being given, and is becoming.

I will join St. Paul, the great apostle of Christ, who simply put it this way: "Christ is all."[1]

In his epistle to the Colossians we hear Paul the mystic visionary who sees what is all in all, not only as individual things present themselves, but also what is beyond, above, beneath, between, and through all. Through and through and through, pulsing with vibrant generativity. Centrifugal, generative force spinning out multiplicity. Gravitational, magnetic, attractional energy synchronizing interconnected quanta. All!

All? Seriously? That seems far too large to swallow. The vibrant and the praiseworthy, perhaps, if we can embrace the mystic's expansive vision of Christ. The glorious glimpses we get of alpenglow on the face of a mountain, yes, or excitement on the face of a child. But: the slug of lead that killed my friend's son? The atomic fission that felled a city? The gene marker muddling the mind of my goddaughter in the prime of her youth? Christ?

All, says Paul: afflictions and glories, slaves and masters, faithful and

We may employ language for abstractions, with analytical precision satisfying to the mind. But we cannot eat an abstraction for breakfast faithless, hostile and embracing, visible and invisible—in his short letter, the apostle mentions these and more in their manifest differences. In Christ God reconciles all things, he claims, "whether things on earth or things in heaven." *All* things!

This is a monumental statement of faith, by which I do not mean a mere doctrinal creed. I mean a trust-fall consent of the human spirit into the divine becoming-oneness of all.

That's all. If it invites and requires *all* of me, well then! That's simple.

For Paul, turns out, it involved "countless floggings… often near death… a stoning… three times shipwrecked… danger from bandits… through many a sleepless night hungry and thirsty… cold and naked."[2] It also involved the joy, happiness, cheerfulness, celebration, and similar sentiments he expressed over 70 times in his letters.[3] In other words, the vast range of human experience, embodied and ensouled in his singular called-upon life.

By "Christ," Paul of Tarsus plainly meant Jesus of Nazareth, a fellow embodied and ensouled singular human being. Paul shared with Jesus an intense spiritual intimacy and communion: "I want to know Christ and the power of his resurrection and the sharing of his sufferings by becoming like him in his death."[4] Paul and Jesus never met in the days Jesus traipsed around Galilee, however, so the epistles make little mention of the sandaled Christ. Christ for Paul is personal, yes, but also transpersonal, transcendent, and divine: "He will transform the body of our humiliation that it may be conformed to the body of his glory."[5] Paul refers to this reality and process of transformation (over 200 times) as being "In Christ."[6] In Christ we experience death and resurrection.[7] In Christ we experience new creation.[8] Not only we humans, but *all things!*

In Christ God reconciles all things, he claims, "whether things on earth or things in heaven." All things!

Is Paul taking us beyond where we are prepared to go? Surely. But we need only a little light, and small steps toward the edge of what we can see.

Prepared or not, you too have lived a life—embodied and ensouled, a narrative unfurling—as did Jesus and Paul. I'll wager you know, deep in your heart, the fellowship of human suffering. You know the hard ache of desolation. You know the stirrings toward newness. You've been dumbstruck by beauty, even if fleeting, and known the seed of beauty's longing planted in your depths. You've known belovedness, and the sweetness of coming home.

In your single precious life you know the great rhythm of the cosmos and its rhyme. "Let us proclaim the mystery of our faith," invites the officiant, holding bread and wine. "Christ has died, Christ is risen, Christ will come again," answer the faithful.

The experience of Christ is the experience of every thing. Franciscan medieval philosophers Duns Scotus and St. Bonaventure spoke of the *univocity* of the divine and the material (sharing "one voice," one essence); the universe is *Christoform.*[9] In its deaths and renewals, the cosmos emanates the Christ-shaped healing and union of all things. Disintegration is woven into the pattern of integration.

You may not have named this Christ. Like any word, it's borrowed and adopted. The term predates Jesus and the apostles, and postdates them in its association with all manner of global and personal atrocities. The Aramaic-speaking gospel writer John borrowed the term *logos* from the Greeks to evoke the inner logic of fundamental reality, the primordial Word of divine creation. John of Patmos speaks of the Alpha and Omega,[10] the beginning and the end: *all.* From every tongue and tribe

Prepared or not, you too have lived a life—embodied and ensouled, a narrative unfurling—as did Jesus and Paul.

and nation there is a lyric. You will have yours.

"Christ plays in ten thousand places," imagines poet Girard Manley Hopkins, "Lovely in limbs, and lovely in eyes not his."[11] Christ is the ever-manifesting embodiment of divine delight, the unfolding of all creation, and the oneness to which it yearns.

Why such poetry? Why such a faith? Anyone might ask, but for my busy crowd there's stuff to be done, and scarcely the time. For activists there are urgencies: blood in the streets, people under bridges, and clients at the door.

If you've ever encountered a longtime, burnt-out, cynical, embittered activist, you know why the soul needs to sing. If you've ever been one yourself, you know even better why. I know, deep in my heart, what happens when the melody and faith fades. I know the hollowness, and the corrosion that spreads through the grinding gears.

I know this firsthand all too well, and thankfully I also know the healing balm of solitude and community that cultivates the loveliness we wish for in the world. I know fullness, flow, and overflow. I know such nourishment invites and requires our very best attention. I know that the tumultuous passages of our fallings and risings, if shepherded well, grow a gritty gracefulness.

I know that we need ears that begin to hear, and eyes that begin to see reality: the being and the becoming, the parts and the whole. The thin place, widening in our field of vision, where human and divine touch; where matter and spirit co-mingle. Christ at play.

We merely *begin* to see, because we dare not claim too much, and wisely learn not to—especially with religious language for realities beyond words. I have already said too much with the language I've got;

Why such poetry? Why such a faith?... For activists there are urgencies: blood in the streets, people under bridges, and clients at the door.

forgive me. I will return to silence presently, my thoughts incomplete. "When the complete comes," envisions the apostle, "the partial will come to an end.... For now we see in a mirror, dimly, but then we will see face to face. Now I know only in part; then I will know fully, even as I have been fully known."[12]

"I am a hole in the flute that Christ's breath moves through," sang the medieval Persian poet Hafez. "Listen to this music."[13] He wrote this of the human person (*per + son = sounding through*), and he could have said it of our city or our planet or a drop of rain. Will we incline our ears and hearts?

Christ is coming—in the world, becoming. It is a dawn beyond our efforts, a future not our own. Can we trust, and give ourselves whole?

—*Scott Dewey*

Our Story

BEYOND OUR EFFORTS

SEEING THINGS AS WE ARE

Mile High Ministries as a Contemplative Activist Community

"We don't see things as they are; we see things as we are."

—Anais Nin

Our spiritual ancestors made cairns from large stones to remind themselves of encounters with God in the wilderness. The prophet Samuel named one such stone *"Ebenezer"* as a reminder of how God's people had been led and protected in a precarious time.[1]

It seems like a good practice. I suppose I might "raise my Ebenezer" on the front porch of a big yellow house on Marion Street, just a few steps from the sometimes-wilderness of Colfax Avenue. I spent Thursday nights there for nearly eight years. The porch was the threshold to Prodigal Coffee House, where dozens of weary and wild homeless teenagers hung out with a little group of overwhelmed volunteers who drank coffee while the kids smoked and told fantastic and painful stories about their lives. Thursday nights—which the kids christened "hippie night" because we spent the last hour singing choruses from a book of classic rock songs—often ended with our unlikely community linking arms and

swaying like a church youth group: "Desperado… you better let somebody love you before it's too late!"

One of my favorite singing desperados first visited Prodigal as a young girl and continued to connect with us through some years of "street-connected" life. She became close to one of our volunteers, and one night had a profound encounter with Christ as the two of them chatted on our porch steps. I asked her later what the experience meant to her. Through tears and sniffles she said, "Well, I believe that if the world ended today I would be with God." Ah, that's so good. "I also believe," she continued, "that angels are throwing a party for me, right now." Yes, she realized her infinite preciousness in God's sight. And she wasn't finished: "And I know that every time a bell rings an angel is getting his wings."

Okay, so maybe she borrowed some of her theology from Clarence in "It's a Wonderful Life." But my young friend was already beginning to see her life differently, learning to tell her difficult story through the lens of God's redeeming love and to trust in God's sustaining presence.[1]

This is my Ebenezer, my written celebration of the ways God has guided us over the past thirty years.

Unleashed

Heidi and I walked into Bear Valley Church as newlyweds in 1983. We had moved to Denver to play in a country-western band, looking to have some fun and to figure out what to do when we grew up.

Nothing about the appearance of the little church on the seam between city and suburbia told us that this was the epicenter of a movement "unleashing" people to give themselves away on behalf of others. Ten years earlier, a young pastor named Frank Tillapaugh began challenging his church to stop referring to pastors as "ministers"—every Christian is a minister, he encouraged, and everyone should prayerfully ask whether God has a place for them on the front lines of ministry outside the walls of the church.

Convinced that suburban middle-class Christians needed relationships that transcend race, class, and culture, Frank pointed his congregation to the needs of the city, and especially the poor.

What had been an inward-focused congregation began reaching out to international students, street people, and refugees. Church members helped start an outreach to homeless people on east Colfax and established "shep-herding homes" for addicts and young moms who wanted to leave street life. One couple gave up half of their suburban medical practice to open the Inner City Health Center. Bear Valley Church became known as a suburban church with "A Heart for the City." Frank's book *Unleashing the Church* was one of the best-selling books of the 1980s on church leadership.

It didn't take long for us to get caught up in the energy. We soon found ourselves, along with our friends in the band, sponsoring a refugee family from Cambodia, setting them up in a subsidized apartment block.

As word about the "church unleashed" spread, pastors from nearby churches asked how they could get involved. A handful of suburban congregations rallied around Open Door Fellowship, a small church serving the street community of Capitol Hill. They created a non-profit organization and started dreaming of ways to work together to reach the poor with the love of Christ: things such as an alternative school, a coffeehouse, backpacking trips for local kids. In 1988 the emerging movement was given a new name: *Mile High Ministries*.

Breaking the Yolk

Our relationship with Cambodian refugees had grown into a small network of people helping refugees from Southeast Asia adjust to life in a new world. While we taught them English, they taught us about resilience in the face of enormous loss, and planted seeds of compassion in our hearts.

Ironically, these new neighbors also introduced us to neighborhoods in the heart of our own city which we might otherwise have been intimidated to visit. My day job as a utilities meter reader also got me walking urban neighborhoods, seeing the city up close and from below. I was becoming a student of the city.

To my surprise, I was offered the job of leading the newborn Mile High Ministries. At the time, it consisted of a handful of disparate programs reaching out to Colfax's street community and to kids from lower-income neighborhoods. Each program was on the verge of being overwhelmed by the chaos of their context, scrambling to find a few dollars to fund their efforts. I was so hungry to lead and to make a difference in the world. Yet, I knew very little about the poor, about leadership, or—significantly—about myself.

Apparently, I couldn't spell, either. We were so eager to tell the world about the big impact Mile High Ministries was going to make that we ordered six-thousand copies of a shiny brochure announcing our plans to "break the yolk of poverty and oppression" in our city, quoting Isaiah 58:6. Sharp readers had fun with the image of churches coming together to crack eggs.

Rescuing the Town Folk

As a young man, I read dozens of western novels by Louis L'Amour. I wanted to be like the heroes in those books: strong, self-sufficient, purging the world of evil through singular acts of courage and dedication. Unlike the world I live in today, cowboy stories don't leave much ambiguity about the good guys (the white hats) and the bad guys (the black hats). And of course, the hero always rides off into the sunset after rescuing the helpless town-folk.

I suppose those stories helped me "cowboy-up" during a few rough scrapes. They also shaped my paradigm for leadership in ways that I would have to unlearn. For one thing, the town-folk weren't so helpless as I had imagined.

I recently found a picture of the basketball team I helped coach at the Denver Street School. One of the guys in the picture was Harold, our team captain. Harold missed a crucial practice the week of the district tournament his senior year. I fumed all day and worked up a plan to lecture him about responsibility and leadership. When I finally reached Harold by phone (pre-cell phone days), he said, "I'm sorry, Coach. My dad and my grandpa got into a fight last night. They both got hurt. The cops put my dad in the psych ward and took my grandpa to jail. I've been running back and forth all day trying to make sure they're both okay." The burden Harold was carrying would have crushed me. That phone conversation was the beginning of my education in what Greg Boyle calls "a compassion that can stand in awe at what [people] have to carry, rather than stand in judgment at how they carry it."[2]

Battleground or Playground?

Not long after taking the reins of Mile High Ministries, I was invited to a presentation by a globally influential leader who was rallying Christians to "take back our cities for God." His approach fit with my Louis L'Amour-inspired paradigm of leadership: the bad guys had taken over the town, and it's our job to take it back (with God's help, of course).

It also fit the way we looked at our Capitol Hill neighborhood, infamous for its debauchery. Openly visible drug-dealing and prostitution were evidence that the bad guys had indeed taken over. To our surprise, the local business district didn't like us religious do-gooders any better than the sex shops that dotted Colfax. In their eyes, street people were still around only because *we* gave them a

reason to stay. We argued with the owner of the business across the street who claimed that "our" street people intimidated his customers. We didn't really care about that, though; after all, it was a bar! When Mayor Webb stopped by on one of his famous walking tours of the city, one of our students rudely heckled him for his support for gays and lesbians; so, he left, disgusted. All of this just confirmed that the city was a battleground, a zero-sum contest between good and evil. Surrounded by hostile forces, we would hold our little piece of turf for God.

In contrast, there is a beautiful image found in the Hebrew scriptures of a city in which those who were once poor now prosper; where children are not destined to misfortune but play safely in the streets under the watchful eye of healthy old men and women; and where all people enjoy communion with God.[3] Significantly, this biblical vision of the city also includes the image of wolf and lamb, lion and ox eating together—rather than eating one another. The city of God's dreams seems to be a place where unlikely partners, even former enemies, live and work together in peace.

Dave Hillis, who directs a global urban network called Leadership Foundations, invites us to see our cities as God's playgrounds—places where all are invited into the

Spirit's ongoing act of creation and the joyous work of redeeming the city of God's dreams. I wish that we had been aware of that image in those early days.[4] Perhaps we would have joined the local business district, eaten lunch at the bar across the street, or asked the mayor how we could help him care for the beautiful diversity of people in our city.

Community Development

Mile High Ministries survived the fragile start-up years. In spite of my inexperience and distorted lenses for seeing the city, I was surrounded by generous, deeply spiritual people, who responded to the poor with acts of compassion that seemed to flow from a source deep within their lives—an inner reality I had not yet experienced. I hoped that if I stuck around and imitated these compassionate friends, something similar would happen within my own heart, that I would live my way into new ways of seeing and thinking.

God sent mentors like John Perkins and Bob Lupton, who were curating a movement of faith-driven leaders living and serving in low-income urban communities across the country. They challenged us to shift our focus from charity to community development: to help reweave the structures of a community and leverage marketplace resources in ways that could make a neighborhood a healthy and supportive place for all people—including our most vulnerable neighbors.

Mile High Ministries folks embraced John's invitation to "relocate" from the suburbs to neighborhoods in the heart of the city. We discovered quickly that in spite of the well-publicized burdens our "inner city" neighborhoods were carrying, the "town-folk" weren't sitting around waiting to be rescued. On our first day in the house where we have lived for twenty-six years, our neighbor Toni told Heidi, "If you're just passing through on the way to something better, you might not be the kind of neighbor we're looking for. But if you're going to take care of your place and help the rest of us take care of the neighborhood, then we're glad to have you here!"

Inspired by our new vision for community development, we went to work! Generous people from churches all over the metro area came together to help turn five large, blighted homes and an abandoned office building on Capitol Hill into a church, an alternative school, a gathering place for people with disabilities, homes of refuge for vulnerable women and children who had been on the streets, counseling offices, dormitories, and office space for non-profit organizations. The 1500 block of Marion Street became a pocket of peace right next door to Colfax Avenue.

The tragic lives—and deaths—of kids we

met at Prodigal Coffee House eventually led us to the motels further east and west along Colfax, where so many vulnerable people were living. "Someone ought to turn one of these awful motels into a decent place for families to live," we said for several years—until it dawned on us that maybe the "someone" was us. Joshua Station began in 2001 when hundreds of volunteers showed up with their tools to turn a blighted Motel 7 into a safe, caring home for families to live and rebuild their lives.

Under the energetic tutelage of volunteer business people, we opened a handful of small businesses to provide jobs, and created a pool of money to make loans to entrepreneurs in our community. Running a non-profit with a social purpose is challenging: building a successful small business is really hard. Doing both at the same time feels… nearly impossible, but worth the effort when you give someone their first real job after a long struggle with addictions or years in prison.

A group of attorneys helped create the Justice and Mercy Legal Aid Center to provide skilled legal help for people struggling with poverty and oppression. At the invitation of local pastors, we opened the Issachar Center for Urban Leadership, and later the Denver Urban Semester, invest in young leaders for the future of our communities.

Denver, Detroit, and Ferguson

At the heart of the activity and generosity has been an abiding trust that we are participating in the love of Christ for our world, and especially for the most vulnerable of our neighbors. Following Jesus into contact with injustice and suffering required us to become students of the city, seeking understanding about race, economics, and urban systems. As we were in the process of learning, people from churches across the metro area have learned with us, joining us for walking tours or workshops. We produced two different video series about life and faith in the city: MetroActive and Urban Entry videos have been shared with people all over the country on topics ranging from homelessness to mass incarceration.

And race. Reckoning with race and racism is a pivotal part of being present and sharing life with our neighbors. Yet even as we lived and served in mostly non-white communities, we confess that a majority of Mile High Ministries' leaders have been white—probably no surprise, given our roots in white, suburban churches.

As early as 1991 a group of non-white pastors graciously invited our board of directors, then comprised entirely of white pastors, to engage in a dialogue about race. It was sometimes difficult for powerful white leaders to recognize the importance of our own racial healing as an end in itself—not solely as a means to accomplishing a program of the church. How patient our friends were when a white pastor tried to explain American history to black pastors. When a Latino pastor said, "We are not here asking for help; we are here as your peers," the process nearly went off the rails. The pastor of a large suburban congregation responded, "If you don't need my help, why should I even be here?"

White America was forced into a renewed attention to race in 1992 when riots broke out in Los Angeles in the wake of the Rodney King verdict. That fall we gathered with John Perkins and the Christian Community Development Association in Detroit for a week of discernment in response to the fresh exposure of America's "original sin" of racism. As we addressed big questions about healing a nation, our own little Mile High Ministries team was sharply divided: arguing about theology, church, politics, and, yes, race. We even had a faction who was angry at me for skipping a session of the conference to see an R-rated movie. (*Last of the Mohicans*, if you're wondering.)

On our final Sunday morning at that Detroit conference, we sat with our backs to one another in a hotel lobby, waiting for a shuttle to the airport. I didn't know how to heal these relational fissures. In fact, I mostly made things worse. Once back home, our little community broke into factions, with nearly everyone angry at me—perhaps my lowest moment as a leader. I almost quit. And yet it's a moment for which I'm profoundly grateful today. Such disorienting times are pregnant with the potential for growth.

I thought back to that difficult season twenty-five years later when a Denver friend filled a van with local leaders for a road trip to Ferguson, Missouri during protests after the killing of Michael Brown by a police officer. I wrote a letter to some of our long-time partners about what I experienced in Ferguson. Although I chose my words carefully, going to Ferguson proved deeply offensive to some of our friends. If I have ever been tempted to think otherwise, Ferguson confirmed for me that race remains the central challenge to the soul of America in its quest to become *e pluribus unum*.

Transformation

"[Cities] are a measure of our ability to live with each other. When we examine our cities we examine ourselves," writes urban geographer John Rennie Short.[5]

This thirty-year "examination" of the city reveals a story of transformation. It's not the transformation of *a city* that we boldly proclaimed in 1988; rather, it's the transformation of *people*—most surprisingly, those of us who respond to the invitation to participate in God's active love for the poor.

Our work is good, helpful, sometimes even dramatically transformative. Yet our role is not as the hero who rides into town to rescue the weak or clean up the mess of a broken city; rather, our vocation is to be present, to share in the life of our city as wounded healers who love, carry, and reconcile what God loves. That vocation places us daily in proximity with injustice and the suffering of our neighbors— sometimes to the point of internalizing their trauma within our own spirits. Yet we have also discovered with Beatrice Bruteau, "the deepest truth is our union with the Absolute, Infinite Being, with God. That's the root of our reality."[6] That's the story being told in and through all of us who are part of the Mile High Ministries family.

Tell It Again

Back on Marion Street, as "hippie night" drew to a close in our living room for homeless youth, a kid whose street-name was Rock pointed out a large painting hanging over the mantle. In the picture, a filthy and bruised young man in rags knelt before a kind-looking older man; the elder's hands were placed tenderly on the young man's shoulders. "Hey, what's that painting about?" Rock asked. I told him, it was the story that gave us the name of our coffeehouse: *Prodigal*. One of our

volunteers, an anesthesiologist from Children's Hospital, offered to tell the story. As he finished and made the connection to God's love for even the most lost among us, the room was unnaturally quiet.

Rock broke the silence. "Damn… that felt GOOD! Tell that story again."

Amen. Tell that story again.

---

1   1 Samuel 7:12

2   Gregory Boyle. *Tattoos on the Heart: The Power of Boundless Compassion* (Free Press, 2010)

3   Isaiah 65:17-25 and Zechariah 8:4-5, among others

4   Dave Hillis. *Cities: Playgrounds or Battlegrounds?: Leadership Foundations' Fifty Year Journey of Social and Spiritual Renewal.* (Leadership Foundations Press, 2014.)

5   John Rennie Short. *The Urban Order: An Introduction to Urban Geography.* (Wiley-Blackwell,1996)

6   Beatrice Bruteau. *Radical Optimism: Practical Spirituality in an Uncertain World.* (Sentient Publications. Boulder, CO. 2002)

MILE HIGH MINISTRIES TIMELINE

EARLY 1980s

Church Unleashed

Pastor Frank Tillapaugh writes *The Church Unleashed*. People from Bear Valley Church in Lakewood become involved in a wide variety of outreach efforts, such as City Lights Coffeehouse, Inner City Health Center, Denver Street School, and the Genesis Center.

1988

MHM is Born

Mile High Ministries (MHM) is born when a handful of other churches partner with Bear Valley Church. Pastors of the churches form the board of directors.

1989

CHAD's

MHM opens its first social enterprise business. CHAD's Boutique hires street-connected kids to operate a trendy resale clothing store.

1990s

Marion Street

Five large houses and an office building on Marion Street just off Colfax—all previously abandoned—are purchased by MHM with down-payment gifts from four churches.

The Community Responds

The network expands when hundreds of volunteers from across Colorado and the nation renovate the Marion Street homes.

The 1500 block of Marion becomes home to:

- **Open Door Fellowship**
- **Denver Street School**, an alternative school
- **TRYAD**, a gathering place for people with disabilities
- **Prodigal Coffee House**, reaching out to street-connected youth
- homes of refuge, counseling offices, volunteer dormitories, and office space

CCDA

We discover a national network of like-minded urban leaders through the Christian Community Development Association (CCDA), founded by John Perkins. We learn from new partners in cities all over the world and help host a week-long national gathering of 2,000 practitioners.

1992

Christmas Store: Inspired by Bob Lupton's model in Atlanta, we explore a more dignifying model for holiday charity. Parents provide presents for their kids by shopping with a steep discount, rather than receiving free toys at a giveaway.

1995

Belay Enterprises

We develop businesses that employ the poor and empower urban entrepreneurs. Our first efforts are Bud's Warehouse and a loan pool for small business owners.

1998

Issachar Center for Urban Leadership

We buy an apartment building in northeast Denver to be a center for equipping a diverse group of young adults for urban Christian leadership through a rigorous program of academics, servant-leadership, and discipleship.

Prodigal opens an outreach on East Colfax in Aurora. We meet families who live in motels, and begin dreaming about creating a safe, healthy alternative.

2000s

International Engagement

Building on partnerships abroad, we help Denver's urban residents venture to Central America, Eastern Europe, West Africa, and East Africa for mutually-supportive learning, service among the poor, and spiritual formation. These experiences grow into long-term, enduring networks of friendship and collaboration.

MetroActive and Urban Entry

We produce a series of training videos that become widely used by churches across the country.

2001

Joshua Station

Seeking to offer safe, transitional housing to families experiencing poverty, we buy the distressed Motel 7 in the Platte Valley. With another massive community effort, we begin renovating the building.

2004

York Street Property

We begin praying regularly about a block of abandoned homes on York Street in the Cole neighborhood, "God, liberate this property!"

2006

JAMLAC

Justice and Mercy Legal Aid Center

We open a legal aid clinic to respond to the need for legal services and representation for people struggling with poverty and oppression.

2007
Denver Urban Semester

We invite college students from across the country to experience a cross-cultural time in the heart of the city, allowing them an opportunity to understand God's unique vocational direction for their life.

2010s
"Contemplative activism"

We find that this phrase captures our way of engaging our city. Examples include:

- **Pilgrimage**—spiritual journeys, locally and nationally, to places of significance and suffering.
- **"A Liturgy of Sacred Sight: Imagining Peace in the Face of Violence"**—gatherings for blessing and reclaiming locations of violence in our neighborhoods.
- **Seeking Peace City Exploration Retreats**—walking tours exploring the connection between contemplation and action in various neighborhoods.

2010
Access

We incubate a spiritual formation community that encourages presence in hard places.

2014
Mile High Workshop

We launch a social enterprise to and train people who are rebuilding from homelessness, addictions, and incarceration—through the manufacture and production of handmade goods.

2015
LIFE

We mentor social work and counseling students in a "Leaders and Interns Formation Experience" that will sustain their calling and work.

Living School

When Father Richard Rohr invites us to partner with The Center for Action and Contemplation (CAC) in Albuquerque, many of our staff and partners begin a two-year program in the Christian contemplative tradition at the CAC's Living School.

2016
Delve Denver Podcast

We highlight the stories of peacemakers in our city.

Clara Brown Commons

After years of prayer, the York Street property in the Cole neighborhood is "liberated" from its long-time owner, giving MHM an opportunity to pursue the dream of a truly affordable housing project and spiritual community.

2018
The Center for Urban Peacemakers

We launch the Center for Urban Peacemakers as a vehicle for training and publishing.

SACRED PLACES OF MILE HIGH MINISTRIES

Where are you?

We often ask this question as we begin a neighborhood walk. The question helps us pay attention to ways that our internal geography intersects with the physical landscape.

After all, we live our lives—including our spiritual lives—in places. Have you considered how your life experience has been shaped by the places where you have lived: your city, your neighborhood, even the actual buildings—houses, apartment buildings, schools, stores, or churches?

The movement of God is an inner reality, a matter of "righteousness, peace, and joy in the Holy Spirit."[1] The inner reality is made manifest in the tangible experiences of life—all of which happen… someplace!

That's why even as we contemplate the inner landscape of the soul, we also pay attention to the built environment that shapes the way we live together. From streets and sidewalks to sewers and schools, from healthcare and housing to policing and public transportation: caring about people requires caring about the places where they live.

One way of tracing the 30-year journey of Mile High Ministries is by remembering places we have camped along the way. Just as people of old piled up cairns of rocks in the wilderness to remind themselves of special encounters with God, these places remind us of the way God brought so many of us together to help create special places in our city—small pockets of peace where people can flourish and where special attention is given to our most vulnerable neighbors.

Ogden Street

Our first location in 1988 was a warehouse on Capitol Hill shared with Open Door Fellowship. The Colfax Street community crowded into City Lights Coffeehouse in the evenings. Denver Street School taught kids on weekdays.

We rented the little storefront next door for our first social enterprise: Chad's Boutique. Today the warehouse is gone. The place that once contained so many of our stories is now empty space, paved over for parking for the nightclub next door. It makes me wonder about the stories of the people who were here before me: where do their stories go when the buildings are bulldozed?

Marion Street

In 1990 MHM bought five large, 100-year-old boarding homes and an office building on Marion Street, just off Colfax Avenue in the heart of Capitol Hill. It was a different time in Denver's real estate market, and the houses were so physically distressed and attracting so much crime that the owners seemed relieved when we offered $100,000 for all five houses!

Over the next five years, hundreds of volunteers lovingly restored these historic structures. Today, Marion Street is home to Open Door Fellowship and Open Door Ministries, providing practical help and hope for people who have experienced poverty and homelessness.

Bud's Warehouse(s)

In 1995 a group of business and ministry leaders created a subsidiary of Mile High Ministries called Belay Enterprises, whose first business was a home-repair thrift store. Bud's Warehouse must have been a lucky charm for landlords, because every rundown warehouse that Bud's rented—901 W. 10th Avenue (Santa Fe), 1309 26th Street (Larimer), and 3350 Brighton Boulevard—eventually got converted into a trendy restaurant, brewery, or apartment complex, reflecting the evolution of Denver's urban core.

Belay became its own corporation many years ago and still provides jobs and training for people facing barriers to full employment in a (finally!) permanent home near I-225 and Mississippi Avenue. Bud's even rents space to the manufacturing operations of another social enterprise that we helped start, the Mile High Workshop.

24th Avenue

In 1999, Mile High Ministries bought and renovated a 75-year old apartment building in northeast Denver's lovely Whittier neighborhood. Many years before that, one of the neighborhood's pastors had traveled to a Christian study center in L'Abri, Switzerland for a season of honest wrestling with life's big questions. Inspired by that idea, the Issachar Center for Urban Leadership was birthed as a kind of "urban L'Abri"—a home and gathering place for young adults from our neighborhood to "understand the times and know what God's people should do."[2]

Wyandot and Mulberry streets

In 2001, hundreds of volunteers showed up with their tools in hand to turn the blighted Motel 7 in the Platte Valley into Joshua Station—a center where families overcome homelessness in a safe and supportive community. Our funky mid-century-modern motel (which bears a striking resemblance to the tragic Lorraine Motel in Memphis where Dr. Martin Luther King, Jr. was assassinated) is found at the intersection of two of Denver's least-recognized streets: Wyandot and Mulberry. You can spot it from the Valley Highway (I-25) by the beautiful turquoise mural that reads "Transforming Families."

The busy interstate and expansive cannabis greenhouses nearby make it hard to imagine that our place near the bank of the South Platte River was once a horse pasture for Camp Weld, a military fort built in 1861 to defend the Union against Confederate plans to capture Colorado's gold fields during the Civil War. Sadly, Camp Weld (see page 131) was also where the 3rd Colorado Cavalry departed in November of 1864 for the tragedy we know as the Sand Creek Massacre.

In 2015 a brand-new building just east of Joshua Station became home to the Justice and Mercy Legal Aid Center. In between these two buildings, in a small patch of green, the Martha Dell Lewis Chapel is a quiet place where all are welcome to pray.

Clara Brown Commons

The Russell Square Apartments were built during World War II for workers at a military supply depot in northeast Denver's Cole neighborhood. For the last three decades they have been essentially abandoned, with a recalcitrant owner defiantly refusing to maintain the property.

Over the last fifteen years people from the Mile High Ministries family have walked the property and prayed: "God, please liberate this property so that it can become something good for the community." Of course, the neighbors had been praying too, as the entire block of vacant buildings attracted violence and crime, a significant blight on an otherwise lovely community.

As we celebrate our 30th year of peacemaking and community development, Mile High Ministries hopes to transform the long-neglected space into a housing community where residents can stabilize their lives, expand their economic capacity, and deepen their spiritual connectedness.

We're renaming the place Clara Brown Commons after a former slave who became a pioneering entrepreneur and philanthropist in Denver history (and one of our Denver Street Saints, whom you can read about on page 44). As a tangible reflection of Clara's example, our goal is to create genuinely affordable housing for more than eighty households, offering residents and neighbors opportunities to belong and build Clara-like lives of resilience, generosity, and self-emptying love.

We are delighted that Clara Brown Commons is located directly across the street from one of our favorite community partners: the Inner City Health Center's roots go back to the same "church unleashed" movement from which Mile High Ministries was born thirty years ago.

———

Heartfelt thanks to all of you who have helped build, support, and enliven these sacred places over the first three decades of our journey!

———

Reflect on your own story by listing some of the places of your life: homes where you have lived; buildings where you have worked; schools you attended; church buildings where you worshipped; or businesses you frequented in various seasons of your life.

Try to remember the physical place in as much detail as you can. Add texture by asking questions like: What was your favorite spot in the building? Who else would have been there with you? What was an especially good memory from that place?

Prepare to be surprised by an emerging awareness of ways that your character and spiritual journey were shaped by these places. (And of course, be kind to yourself should some of these places generate painful memories.)

—Jeff Johnsen

1   Romans 14:17
2   1 Chronicles 12:32

WHAT, WHY, AND HOW
The Mission, Vision, and Values of Mile High Ministries

What do we do? (Our Mission)

We seek God's peace for our city through the creative, compassionate, and prayerful development of people and communities.

Why do we do what we do? (Our Vision)

Our vision is for Denver to be a city where those who were once poor enjoy the fruit of their labor; where children of the city are no longer doomed to misfortune, but play safely in the streets under the watchful eye of healthy old men and women; where former rivals and natural enemies live and work together in peace; and where all people enjoy the experience of communion with God. This vision draws its inspiration from the breathtaking image of a city of joy found in the scriptures of our faith.[1]

How do we go about our work? (Our Values)

As we have reflected on three decades of Mile High Ministries, a handful of guiding values has emerged. Miraculously, every one of them starts with the letter P! (Well okay, maybe it wasn't a miracle: we might have rigged the outcome just a little to make the list catchier.) Anyway, we call these eight ideas our "organizational proverbs" and they do help guide the way we try to live as a community.

---

1   E.g. Isaiah 65:17-25 and Zechariah 8:4-5

Presence

It starts with the story of God's presence among us, fully alive in the human experience—a story that invites us to be fully present as well, as we share life with our neighbors. If we are vessels of hope and healing, we are certainly broken vessels, wounded healers. Availability and vulnerability are often the only gifts we have to share with others—and those gifts are often more than enough.

Prayer

"You can only act within the world that you can see." One of the most helpful ways we know to focus our sight and to shape how we see is to pray. Prayer takes different forms within the Christian tradition. Appreciating diversity and honoring the various paths to God, we find ourselves increasingly drawn towards contemplation. We are learning the value of quieting our hearts and minds to listen for the voice of God and rest in divine love. Prayer is itself a kind of presence: being present to God; trusting that God is fully present to us.

Peacemaking

"Blessed are the peacemakers," Jesus said, "for they shall be called children of God."[2] Peacemaking is about relationship and collaboration, including with unlikely partners who might see the world differently than we do—for the shared joy of building healthy and welcoming communities. We seek to practice a non-dual consciousness free from the ruts of rivalries—a way of being that liberates people and communities from labels and invites us all into compassionate engagement.

2   Matthew 5:9

Place

The movement of God is an inner reality, a matter of "righteousness, peace, and joy in the Holy Spirit."[3] Yet, this inner reality is made manifest in the tangible experiences of life—all of which happen... someplace! That's why even as we contemplate the inner landscape of the soul, we also pay attention to the built environment that shapes the way we live together—from streets and sidewalks, to sewers and schools. Caring about people means caring about the places where they live. Placemaking is a piece of pursuing *shalom*—creating places where all people are included and given opportunities to flourish together.

Playground

Let's be honest, sometimes as religious folks or activists we are too quick to see the city as a battleground between good and evil—where everything becomes a win/lose proposition, filled with zero-sum competitions and endless rivalries. We are learning to see the city as a *playground*—a deeper reality than "us versus them."[4] Playgrounds are open spaces where there is the freedom to form new teams, to try new things, and even to fail.

Power

We hope to imitate the way Jesus used his power, not clinging to self-validation or importance, but "emptying the self" to enter fully into a humble place of powerlessness and vulnerability. It appears that it will take a lifetime of suffering and love to learn the art of *kenosis* (self-emptying).

Meanwhile, though it may be a buzzword, we also try to put our best efforts into building communities where people experience *empowerment*—the expanded capacity to shape their own lives. Sharing power

---

3   Romans 14:17
4   We are grateful to Dave Hillis and Leadership Foundations for teaching and modeling this way of seeing the city.

and making space for indigenous leadership is a lifegiving challenge in our diverse community.

Plenty

Peacemaking is rooted in an asset-based vision of life, trusting that there is enough—enough of all the ingredients for human flourishing. Our task is to pay attention to how the Spirit is already at work in our world and joyfully participate in unleashing forces for good. We are trying to figure out what it looks like to pursue practical strategies of community development that are rooted in this vision of an abundant, asset-based lifestyle.

Prophetic Imagination

Prophets of old told stories, wrote poetry, and lived in peculiar ways that called out the idolatry and injustice of their day. We sense a call to name and engage the idolatry and injustice of our own time and place. The needed twist in our time is to do that without projecting our anxiety and fear onto neighbors who might see the world differently than we do.

A few pics
from Mile High
Ministries

Resources

BEYOND OUR EFFORTS

GOD IN OUR EVERYDAY LIVES
Praying the Examen

As contemplative activists engaged with vulnerable people and communities, we seek prayers that guide us into daily awareness of God's abundant goodness. Saint Ignatius of Loyola, of the 16th century, offers us one such practice in the prayer of The Examen.

The Examen can be prayed individually—often times at the end of each day—or with a community. Although there is freedom and variety in the way the Daily Examen is undertaken, most approaches include the following movements:

❖ **Become aware of God's presence.** Look back on the events of the day, asking God to bring clarity and understanding.

❖ **Review the day with gratitude.** Note its joys and gifts. Life is filled with God. Look at your work, the people you interacted with, and even small moments.

❖ **Pay attention to your emotions and their movements.** What is God saying through these feelings?

❖ **Choose one experience of the day to pray about.** Allow the prayer to arise spontaneously from your heart—whether intercession, praise, repentance, or gratitude.

❖ **Look toward tomorrow.** Ask God to give you light for tomorrow's challenges. Pray for hope.

A Guide for Praying the Examen in Community

❖ Prayer

Gracious God, Creator, Redeemer, and Sustainer of Life, have mercy on us. Reveal yourself in all things, to all things, and through all things. Grant us the gift of becoming a community of Christ-like desire who sees and celebrates good news in hard places.

❖ Invocation

Come, Holy Spirit. Quiet our souls. Teach us how to pray. Be our guide, our counselor, our advocate, and our defender. Speak to us again the truth of our deepest identity hidden in you: "You are my sons and daughters whom I love."

❖ Presence

You are Immanuel—the God who is with us. There is nowhere we can flee from your presence, and nothing can separate us from your love. We accept your invitation to relax into this miracle—to notice and to welcome your presence in all things.

We name your presence in places where it is particularly needed and hard to see…

We name places where your presence is clearly visible…

❖ Gratitude

The deepest form of gratitude we can offer is our own joy. We recognize that your presence is the substance of all that we hope for.

As we learn to trust our deepest desires, we give thanks for…

❖ Gift of the Spirit

We welcome you, Holy Spirit. Give us courage and compassion to see ourselves, our relationships, our world, and even our enemies as we really are. Ease the fear that blinds us, binds us to our false selves, and keeps us from the truth that sets us free.

Spirit, we receive your light in the movements of our emotions, naming these today…

❖ Reflection

As those who are being renewed by your love, we freely confess to you the deep wounds of blindness, voicelessness, despair, and isolation. We confess our misplaced desires that bind us to our wounds in deceptive and destructive ways. Re-create us as manifestations of your unfolding desire, that we might discover ourselves again in you. Lord have mercy; Christ have mercy.

For ourselves and our communities we confess and acknowledge…

❖ Resolve

As your beloved ones who are forgiven and free, we freely forgive those who have done harm. May we break the chains of injustice that hold your children captive. May we be midwives to the holy as we seek the peace of our communities. May we gladly participate in the ongoing act of creation, expressing your lavish beauty in our daily work and play. Gracious God, we ask for grace: to do and to will your good pleasure. Lord have mercy.

As your Spirit leads, we resolve to...

❖ Our Lord's Prayer

Our Father who is in heaven, holy is your name. May your kingdom come and your will be done on earth as it is in heaven. Give us this day our daily bread; and forgive us our sins, as we forgive those who sin against us. Lead us not into temptation, but deliver us from evil. For yours is the kingdom, and the power, and the glory forever. Amen.

❖ Benediction

The Spirit of the Lord is upon us, because as followers of Jesus the Anointed One, we too have been anointed to preach good news to the poor—to proclaim release to the captives and recovery of sight to the blind, to let the oppressed go free, and to proclaim the year of the Lord's favor. We pray all of this in the name of the Father who is for us, the Son who is with us, and the Spirit who unites us all in the never-ending dance of love. Amen.

This version was adapted by the Street Psalms Community from the Daily Examen by St. Ignatius of Loyola (1491-1556)

LONG WANDERING PRAYER
Invitation to Walk with God

The Long Wandering Prayer happens on the inside like it happens on the outside. It is long in prayer and long in wandering with God. We aspire to embrace long prayer with the faith and hope that it will make changes in ourselves and our world.

This spiritual practice is as simple as it sounds. It involves walking and pausing as we desire, to contemplate lily, tree, or bird—cloud, sunset, or moon. This prayer helps our naturally wandering minds to see and listen with newness.

Writer Rebecca Solnit calls walking "the intentional act closest to the unwilled rhythms of the body, to breathing and the beating of the heart."[1]

As the Psalmist prays, "I want to drink God, deep draughts of God. I'm thirsty for God-alive."[2] Long Wandering Prayer allows for deeper communion with God. We step away from our normal, fast-moving environment, take God's hand, and spend hours meeting and talking in the park, at the lake, or mountains.

Take a prayer walk with God today.

---

1 Rebecca Solnit. Wanderlust: *A History of Walking* (Penguin Books 2001)
2 Psalm 42:2 (The Message)

THE WELCOMING PRAYER

Welcome, welcome, welcome.
I welcome everything that comes to me today
because I know it's for my healing.
I welcome all thoughts, feelings, emotions, persons,
situations, and conditions.
I let go of my desire for power and control.
I let go of my desire for affection, esteem,
approval, and pleasure.
I let go of my desire for survival and security.
I let go of my desire to change any situation, condition,
person, or myself.
I open to the love and presence of God and
God's healing action within.
Amen.

Welcoming Prayer is a practice of "attending, letting go, and surrendering to God in the present moment of daily life."[1] It was developed and taught in this form by Mary Mrozowski (1925-1993), a founding member of Contemplative Outreach, with each phrase carefully representing key challenges and opportunities of the soul.

Welcoming Prayer has been an ongoing gift to our community, guiding us to sit with our hardest and most real emotions. Our work is challenging, and life is full of twists and turns that are often unexpected. These realities offer us all a choice: to welcome healthy engagement with our inner turmoil, or to repress and resist the emotions that arise.

Choosing to face our feelings allows each of us—as lawyers, social workers, administrators, chaplains, and as human beings—to pay attention to what our circumstances are producing in our spirits. We are invited to open ourselves up to God in the midst of situations and conditions that are unfavorable, unenjoyable, and even profoundly unjust.

By pausing to pray this prayer we stand in a grounded place and allow ourselves to embrace these moments and then let them go. We choose freedom over attachment and control.

As Cynthia Bourgeault teaches, this practice of surrender is not passive, but rather it is "the active exercise of a receptive power."[2]

—Rebecca Mendoza Nunziato

---

1   https://www.contemplativeoutreach.org/article/concern-about-welcoming-prayer-and-passivity December 12, 2018

2   Ibid.

EUCHARIST LITURGY

*"It is with desire I have desired to eat this Passover meal with you
before I suffer." Luke 22:15*

Greeting

(Servant): Peace be with you.

(All): And also with you.

Centering Prayer

(All): Lord, we are hungry and thirsty for life.

Assurance

(S): God of all life everywhere, you have been the stranger among us, preparing this meal since the foundations of the world. You have declared this meal your eternal joy. It is the meal that reconciles all of creation. It is the never-ending meal, ever-extending to a hungry and hurting world. Here, at this meal, you have declared that there is enough for all and there is room for all. It is the sign of your peace into which we now enter.

(A): Lamb of God, you take away the sins of the world; have mercy on us. Lamb of God, you take away the sins of the world; have mercy on us. Lamb of God, you take away the sins of the world; grant us peace.

(S): You said, "Peace I leave with you; my peace I give to you. I do not give to you as the world gives. Do not let your hearts be troubled, and do not let them be afraid."

(A): Lord, make us instruments of your peace.

Confession

(Women): Jesus, we come to the table having tasted the reality of your goodness and the mystery of your abundant love. We also come having tasted the bitterness of our own sin and the sin of others. We are part of a love-starved world that craves that which cannot satisfy. You've happily let go of all our sin long, long ago, and yet we drag it to the table with us, unsure of how to live without it. We come to the table tempted to stuff ourselves in fear or starve ourselves in shame. Lord, help us.

(Men): Forgive us for all the ways we diminish the meal you have provided; for all the ways we are ruled by myths of scarcity; for all the ways we grumble at the table; for all the ways we guard against your mercy and withhold it from others; for all of our misplaced and displaced desires that have caused so much harm.

(A): Heal us, O Lord.

Words of Institution

(S): On the night that Jesus was betrayed, he took bread, blessed it, broke it, gave it to his disciples, and said, "Take and eat; this is my body, broken for you. Do this in remembrance of me." In the same way, after supper, he took the cup, blessed it, gave it for all to drink, and said, "This cup is the blood of the new covenant, shed for you and for all people for the forgiveness of sin. Do this in remembrance of me." The Apostle Paul adds, "For as often as we eat of this bread and drink from this cup, we proclaim the Lord's death until he comes."

Paschal Mystery

(A): Christ has died. Christ is risen. Christ will come again.

Contemplations

(S): As the body of Christ in the world, we not only partake of the meal, we also become part of the meal of which we partake. The Eucharist inducts us into reality and reveals its hidden pattern at work in our lives, as we are taken, blessed, broken, given, and spoken.

(M): We are *taken* into the loving hands of God. Let us feast on God's love as the foundation of all life and transformation. All of creation is taken into the love from which it comes.

(W): In the loving hands of God, we are *blessed*. Let us drink deeply of the incarnation and creation in Christ as the blessing of God's presence in the world.

(M): We are *broken* in and through the love of God. Let us taste God's own experience of suffering on the cross, and how that experience transforms death into life.

(W): As broken ones, we are *given* to a broken world. Let us savor life inside of the resurrection and its gift to the world.

(A): All of life is *spoken* into existence through this meal. Let us digest the living Word that speaks all of life into existence.

Receiving the Elements

Our Lord's Prayer

(A): Our Father who is in heaven, holy is your name. May your kingdom come and your will be done on earth as it is in heaven. Give us this day our daily bread; and forgive us our sins, as we forgive those who sin against us. Lead us not into temptation, but deliver us from evil.

For yours is the kingdom, and the power, and the glory forever. Amen.

Benediction

(S): "When Jesus was at the table with them, he took bread, blessed and broke it, and gave it to them. Then their eyes were opened, and they recognized him."

(A): Like the disciples who were blind to your presence until they dined with you in the resurrection, we too are blind to your presence until you dine with us. You are the stranger among us, revealed as the loving host of the meal of our salvation. Open our eyes, Lord, to the stranger among us. We want to see and celebrate you at work in the world—creating, sustaining, and uniting all of creation in the meal of our salvation.

We pray all of this in the name of the Father and Mother who is for us, the Son who is with us, and the Spirit who unites us all in the never-ending dance of love. Amen.

(S): Go in peace.

In a time of intense division over ideologies, political and theological, it is shared practice that offers the possibility for people of good faith and good will to come together. Loving concern for our most vulnerable neighbors is certainly among the best of such possibilities. So is Eucharist, or the Lord's Table. That's why this celebration is such a meaningful part of the life of Mile High Ministries. This expression of the Eucharist, emphasizing five verbs found within the heart of the meal, is drawn from the book ***Meal from Below*** by our own Scott Dewey and our friend Kris Rocke (Street Psalms Press, 2012).

* Note: The wording "with desire I have desired" is a literal rendering of the original Greek text of Luke 22:15. The double intensive emphasizes the depth of Jesus's desire for communion with his friends at the meal. Other scripture sources: Greeting (John 20:21), Assurance (John 1:29, 14:27), Confession (Isa. 55:1-2; Matt. 8:8), Words of Institution (1 Cor. 11:23-26), Lord's Prayer (Matt. 6:9-13), Benediction (Luke 24:30-31).

TEN DAYS OF PRAYER GUIDE
Opening Our Hearts Among the Vulnerable

Housing

"I am so grateful for my home. It symbolizes independence and a new beginning on my own."
—Nicole

Home represents rest, the love of family, and a refuge where we are free to be ourselves.

Many homeless people in Denver are unable to find a peaceful place to rest, free from harassment from police officers, gangs, or other homeless people. This lack of quality rest makes it hard to stay physically and mentally well. Jesus says, "Come to me, all you who are weary and burdened, and I will give you rest."[1]

Prayer: As you enter your home after a long day of work, dwell on the blessing of housing. Hear God's message of grace and affection as you give thanks for safety, shelter, and comfort. Pray for the homeless, and pray for opportunities to embody Jesus's words by offering those who are weary a place to rest.

---

1   Matthew 11:28

Day 2

Faith

Times of crisis both challenge our faith and call us to new ways of engaging it. Since leaving the streets, Margo has selflessly volunteered to help others and encourage them in their faith journeys.

"Faith doesn't mean everything is gonna get easy. I'm grateful for faith because that's the only thing that kept me going on the streets."
—Margo

Prayer: Consider those who help guide and develop your faith. Give thanks for them and pray that God may help you encourage others to access the gift of faith. Pray for compassionate mentors and agents of hope who help people transform bondage into freedom. Pray for those who feel that they have nothing left but faith.

Day 3

Family

"I'm grateful for my kids. Having them here keeps me going." —Mary

Although Mary remains homeless (which means maintaining custody of her children is often tenuous), her words remind us of the life-giving power of family. Family serves as the river that reminds us of who we have been, and keeps us moving into who we might become.

Prayer: Today, allow God to help you see your family through fresh eyes. Celebrate these loved ones and give thanks for the gift of their presence. Pray for those you know (perhaps you?) who need... healing in places of family brokenness.

Day 4

Employment

Over 500 individuals are released from jail or prison monthly in the Denver metropolitan area. Out of that population, nearly 50% will end up reincarcerated.[2] At Mile High Workshop, through job training and counseling, people are given a chance to overcome these odds. Of employees that stay with MHW for at least 60 days, 86% move on to a permanent job.[3]

"Recently my probation was lifted, allowing light to shine as I begin working a part-time job for the first time in my life." —Matt

Matt and his wife deeply appreciate this gift of employment, which is leading them toward greater ability to provide for their four children.

Prayer: Many of us have had multiple jobs throughout our lives. Reflect on the employment opportunities you have had and be grateful for who they have allowed you to become. Pray for your co-workers to find joy in their lives and work. Pray for those who seek work and for those who are unable to succeed in a traditional employment environment.

2   https://www.colorado.gov/pacific/cdoc/departmental-reports-and-statistics November 28, 2018

3   https://www.milehighworkshop.org/impact/October 1, 2018

Education

"I'm thankful to be in college. No one from my family has ever finished college." —Angela

Regardless of the level of education, a completed degree opens a portal of opportunity, moving us forward into our future. Our lives are enhanced through learning. Yet studies show that in Denver American Indian, Hispanic, and black students graduate less often than their peers from other racial and ethnic backgrounds.[4]

Within Denver Public Schools over 33,000 students are learning English as a second language.[5] Think of the children of immigrants and refugees adjusting to a new way of life, learning a new language, and learning to read!

Prayer: Take a moment to reflect on the most influential educators in your journey, and acknowledge how God has woven these people's dedication and gifts into the tapestry of your life. Pray for the children of the world who live and study in Denver—from Somalia, Vietnam, Mexico, Nepal, and beyond. Pray for non-traditional students finishing a GED or going to trade school to better themselves and their families.

4   https://www.denvergov.org/content/dam/denvergov/Portals/713/documents/2014_Data--Lisa/DPS%20Fact%20Sheet.pdf October 1, 2018
5   Ibid..

Healthcare

For some of us, it's hard to imagine having limited or nonexistent healthcare. Our ability to live our everyday lives is, in many ways, directly thanks to the skill of medical professionals. In our city, Denver Health serves over 210,000 unique patients every year and cares specifically for "the poor, uninsured, pregnant teens, persons addicted to alcohol and other substances, victims of violence, and the homeless."[6]

"My nurses are angels. I feel so thankful and cared for. I know that I would have already died if I were not in America." —Tina

Prayer: Take a deep breath and pay careful attention to the state of your physical body. Remember the individuals who have provided you with care throughout your life. Give thanks to the Great Physician for your physical health. Pray for the sick in our city.

6   https://www.denverhealth.org/about-denver-health December 12, 2018

Day 7

Transportation

For many of our neighbors, reliable transportation is synonymous with empowerment. For those in poverty, reliable and efficient transportation could play a significant role in improving their families' lives; but it is often inaccessible.

"I am so excited and thankful to finally have a car. It has been so difficult getting to all our appointments on the bus." —Meghan

Prayer: This week when you arrive at your destination, whether your job or the grocery store, pause. Take five seconds to be grateful for transportation. Ask a blessing for those who struggle with transportation, and consider providing it when you notice them.

Day 8

Citizenship

"I am thankful for inner peace to realize my dreams. I have carried this sense of peace since the day I received my permanent residency papers." —Karen

As our friend Karen describes, being welcomed as a permanent resident in the United States allows her to experience a refreshing new freedom. Denver ranks among the 20 U.S. metro areas with the largest numbers of undocumented people.[7] Consider the challenges these families experience and the ways they are vulnerable to violence and mistreatment. Notice those who clean our schools, cars, and offices; notice those who work the fields—and bless them.

Prayer: God has extended welcome to each of us, affirming our belonging. Pray that we each may open our arms to the stranger. Make your prayer active by creative ways of saying and showing, "Welcome!"

---

7   https://www.denverpost.com/2017/02/09/denver-illegal-population/
October 1, 2018

 **Day 9**

Food

"I am so grateful for this food. I can't believe that we are so blessed. What more can we ask for? In my country no one would help those people who did not have food." —Mohamed

"Give us this day our daily bread."[8] Following Jesus's model, we often pause at mealtime to acknowledge divine sustenance. Like the other necessities that we've mentioned, our daily need for food offers the opportunity to be mindful of simple blessings; each meal can become a celebration.

In Denver, delight in the diversity of food with a visit to an ethnic restaurant such as Axum, an Ethiopian restaurant on East Colfax, Saigon Bowl off Federal Blvd., or Chubby's on the North Side.

Prayer: Whether through the sacramental elements of bread and wine or through the beauty of a backyard BBQ, we invite you to communion today. Gather together in a communal practice of gratitude for everyday blessings. Pause to taste the goodness. Pray for those who hunger and thirst.

---

8   Matthew 6:11

Day 10

Blessing

"As I pray each day with a grateful heart, my life and my relationship with God and others in my world has grown deeper." —Ben

Gratitude transforms our hearts; it prompts action. We are often moved by the sacrificial generosity of the poor. What are the proactive ways we can express gratitude to God for the blessings we receive?

Prayer: After Jesus provided healing or restoration, he often sent an individual or group out to express their thanks by creatively blessing others. Pray that God would provoke our imaginations, as well as our hands and feet, to share with and bless others in our ordinary, everyday living.

These prayers were developed by Ryan Taylor, Director of Network Coffeehouse in Denver. The Mile High Ministries community has prayed and shared them with our own network to help all of us—and especially those who enjoy an abundance of housing, food, medical care, family, and education—deepen compassion for our neighbors who long to have these needs met in their lives.

LITURGY OF SACRED SIGHT
Imagining Peace in the Face of Violence

Date: _____   Location: _____

Greeting

Leader: Grace and peace to all in the name of our loving God. This space that was traumatized by senseless violence, we reclaim as a place of life, community, and hope. We welcome all persons, all conditions, and all emotions to this gathering—as we trust the process of love and healing within and around us.

What We Know About This Tragedy

Leader: (read details gathered from media reports, loved ones, and other sources)

Declaration

Leader: We come together in this space and at this time of grief, acknowledging the tragic loss of our neighbor. We confess that this tragedy is part of a wider failure of community. We long for communities where everyone can belong, feel safe, and experience the simple dignity of respect for their life as a fellow human being. As individuals and as a community, we hold a creative tension between grief and resolve. In trust, we release what we cannot hold or control. In faithful resolve to action, we humbly ask the question, "What is mine to do?"

Psalm 23

Leader: The Lord is our shepherd.

ALL: **We lack nothing.**

Leader: The Lord makes us lie down in green pastures.

ALL: **The Lord leads us beside still waters.**

Leader: The Lord restores our soul.

ALL: **The Lord guides us in right paths.**

Leader: Even though we walk through the valley of the shadow of death.

ALL: **We will fear no evil, for You are with us. Your rod and staff give us courage.**

Beatitudes *(from Matthew 5)*

Leader: Blessed are the poor in spirit.

ALL: **For theirs is the kingdom of heaven.**

Leader: Blessed are those who mourn.

ALL: **For they will be comforted.**

Leader: Blessed are the meek.

ALL: **For they shall inherit the earth.**

Leader: Blessed are those who hunger and thirst for righteousness.

ALL: **For they shall be satisfied.**

Leader: Blessed are the merciful.

ALL: **For they shall obtain mercy.**

Leader: Blessed are the pure in heart.

ALL: **For they shall see God.**

Leader: Blessed are the peacemakers.

ALL: **For they shall be called children of God.**

Leader: Blessed are those who are persecuted for the sake of justice.

ALL: **For theirs is the kingdom of heaven.**

A Time of Sharing

Leader: What are we seeing, hearing, and feeling in this moment?
(participants may share out loud briefly)

Affirmation of Sight

ALL: Our (brother/sister) _____ *[first name],* we see you. We acknowledge your death and your life. You did not leave this world unseen. We hold your memory in our love and care. We affirm that your life was and is treasured by God.

Prayer

Leader: Spirit, we offer our hearts to you as we pray the words of the Psalmist:

ALL (pause to take 2–3 deep breaths between each line):

Be still & know that I am God.

Be still & know that I am.

Be still & know.

Be still.

Be.

Litany of Deliverance

Leader: From the brutality of murder and violence

ALL: **Save us, O God**

Leader: From injustice and oppression

ALL: **Save us, O God**

Leader: From the hopelessness of suicide

ALL: **Save us, O God**

Leader:	From the ravages of drug and alcohol addiction
ALL:	**Save us, O God**
Leader:	From the snare of mental illness and despair
ALL:	**Save us, O God**
Leader:	From the bitterness of homelessness and empty pockets
ALL:	**Save us, O God**
Leader:	From the arrogance of racism and all discrimination
ALL	**Save us, O God**
Leader:	From the lie of scarcity
ALL:	**Save us, O God**
Leader:	From the silence of apathy and neglect
ALL:	**Save us, O God**
Leader:	From the selfishness of "not in my back yard"
ALL:	**Save us, O God**
Leader:	From the many ways human dignity is stripped
ALL:	**Save us, O God**
Leader:	And from all evil….
ALL:	**Save us, O God**
Leader:	And from all evil….
ALL:	**Save us, O God**
Leader:	And from all evil….
ALL:	**Save us, O God**
ALL:	Amen

Water Ceremony—*A Reclaiming Ritual*

Leader: We come together this day to reclaim this space of violence as a place of healing and peace. This place that has been subjected to fear, anger, and pain, we reclaim for the world as a place of hope and community.

Leader (using a branch of leaves or other object gathered from the location, water is sprinkled on those present, as the leader reads these words):

As we sprinkle this water, we recognize you, Holy Spirit, in this place. Redeem this space and community from the pain and loss that occurred here. Return it as a safe place, a place of love, a place of life, a place of hope. Amen.

ALL: **That which was taken away from us by violence and death, we reclaim as a place of life, community, and hope. We pledge to work toward a world free from violence and oppression, full of love and kinship. We commit ourselves to building community that is humane, compassionate, just, and filled with dignity.**

Neighborhood Blessing

Leader: What is a blessing but a rain of grace falling generously into the lives of those in need; and what neighborhood in this city is without need?

ALL: **God, we ask your blessing on this neighborhood of _____.**

Leader: May the Spirit touch _____ *[this neighborhood]* in this morning pause. May this day provide a pathway filled with hope and renewal. May there be work today in _____ *[this neighborhood]* that is God's love made visible.

ALL: **God, we ask your blessing on this neighborhood.**

Leader: May a heart of grace and benevolence be born here today. And may that birth bless each person in this community with hope for the future.

ALL: **God, we ask your blessing on this neighborhood.**

Leader: May the resurrection be experienced in _____ *[this neighborhood]* today. As old enemies are moved toward reconciliation, exclusion becomes embrace, and voices of criticism and hate are transformed into encouragement.

ALL: **God, we ask your blessing on this neighborhood.**

Leader: May greed and excess dissolve into the soil of community gardens where neighbors and families share meals together and where children are free to play and explore their curiosities.

ALL: **God, we ask your blessing on this neighborhood.**

Leader: God, breathe upon _____ *[this neighborhood]* so when her people look in the mirror, they may see themselves as they truly are... a beautiful reflection of you.

ALL: **God, we ask your blessing on our city. Amen.**

Scripture Reading *(adapted from Isaiah 61)*

Leader: The Spirit of the sovereign Lord is on us,
because the Lord has anointed us
to proclaim good news to the poor.
God has sent us to bind up the brokenhearted
to proclaim freedom for the captives
and release from darkness for the prisoners,
to proclaim the year of the Lord's favor,
to comfort all who mourn,
and provide for those who grieve in Zion—

to bestow on them a crown of beauty instead of ashes, the oil of
joy instead of mourning, and a garment of praise instead of a
spirit of despair.
They will be called oaks of righteousness,
a planting of the Lord for the display of the Lord's splendor.

Affirmation of Our Worth

All: **We are made in God's image.**
We are made of love, not shame.
We are never alone.
Christ is with us.
Do not be afraid.

Benediction

Leader: Beloved of God, this concludes our Liturgy of Sacred Sight. May
we go forth in the name of the Father who is for us, the Son who is
with us, and the Spirit who unites us all in the never-ending dance
of love. Amen.

This liturgy is shared by an informal network of friends who gather when someone
dies violently near one of our homes, churches, workplaces, or other places we share
life connection. First developed during a violent season in Tacoma, Washington, the
ceremony has been adapted by a small international collective called Street Psalms for
prayer in neighborhoods from Nairobi to Guatemala City to Camden, New Jersey—and
Denver. See the "Public Action" essay in the Winter section of this book (p. 54) for a
deeper exploration.

A PRAYER FOR OUR CITY AND CITIES OF THE WORLD

Loving God, you have set us in families and clans, in cities and neighborhoods.

Our common life began in a garden, but our destiny lies in the city.

You have placed us in Denver. This is our home.

Your creativity is on display here through the work of human hearts and hands.

We pray for Denver today—for the East Side; West Side; North and South.

For Montbello, Sun Valley, Green Valley, and all 26 miles of Colfax.

We pray for our poorest neighbors, and for powerful people in banks and offices downtown.

We pray for people from the 'hood and the barrio, and for the new urbanites.

We pray for Denver's sisters: Aurora, Arvada, Cherry Hills, Lakewood, Thornton, Highlands Ranch, and others.

And for Albuquerque and Cheyenne, Jerusalem and Nairobi, Kunming and Cuernavaca—and a thousand other cities connected to our own.

In all our neighborhoods this day there will be crime and callous moneymaking; there will be powerful people unable or unwilling to see the vulnerable who are their neighbors.

There will also be beautiful acts of compassion and creativity in all these places—forgiveness and generosity; neighbors working together for a more just community.

Help us see this place as something other than a battleground between us and them, where our imaginations are limited by win/lose propositions and endless rivalry.

Show us a deeper reality, God: show us your playground, and invite us to play.

Like the city of your dreams, make this a city where those who were once poor enjoy the fruit of their labor;

A place where children are no longer doomed to misfortune, but play safely in the streets under the watchful eye of healthy old men and women;

A place where former rivals and natural enemies work and play together in peace;

And where all people enjoy communion with you. We pray in the name of the one who wept over the city. Amen.

This prayer may be read responsively in a group with a leader and respondents. It is adapted from Walter Brueggemann's *Prayers for a Privileged People* (Abingdon Press, 2010). We pray it during walks through the neighborhoods of our city.

CONTRIBUTORS

About Us

Beyond Our Efforts has been a shared endeavor involving the Mile High Ministries team. A small group—the "primary authors" listed below—worked at it for a couple of years. Special thanks to Scott Dewey and Rebecca Nunziato, whose loving expertise and long hours made each piece and the whole book better.

Thanks to the generosity of Father Richard Rohr, many of our staff members—including most of those who wrote for this book—are students in the Living School for Center for Action and Contemplation in Albuquerque. The fingerprints of that experience can be found throughout the book.

Primary Authors and Editors

Jeff Johnsen, AKA the Urban Cowboy, left rural Colorado to play western music in the big city of Denver with his wife Heidi. He has been the executive director of Mile High Ministries since its founding in 1988 and lives in northeast Denver with his family. On rare occasions, Jeff still serves up a lonesome cowboy yodel for his friends.

Scott Dewey is a chaplain and spiritual director—especially for those in the challenging contexts of poverty and trauma survival. He's been part of the Mile High Ministries team in various capacities for 25 years. Through our affiliate program Centering Way, Scott helps people "tend to the soul" in Denver, Romania and elsewhere in the world. When he can, he goes fly fishing—ask him about the magical world of insects.

Rebecca Mendoza Nunziato is our reggaetón beat loving hippy Latina. She types on her 1940s Royal Quiet Deluxe Typewriter before bed in the RV dwelling she shares with her husband and hedgehog. Rebecca directs Mile High Ministries' Center for Urban Peacemakers, and her favorite day consists of thrift stores, coffee shops and poetry.

Scott Jenkins, who we call Padre, is the chaplain of our staff. Father Scott is a former pastor, a trained hostage negotiator, and a spiritual director. He founded Celtic Way to teach and encourage people in a creation-based experience of following Christ. He's also a great-grandpa.

Penny Salazar-Phillips has 40 years on the front lines of counseling and social work, focusing on grief and helping women heal from trauma. Penny now directs LIFE—mentoring future social workers, chaplains and counselors. She is the creative force who we turn to fill any room with meaning and beauty. She lives near Sloan's Lake, where she is the first to spot the return of pelicans each Spring.

Contributors

Marlene Bedoya has a diverse background including communications, real estate, and foreign relations. She serves as Justice and Mercy Legal Aid Center's liaison to the Denver Hispanic community. Marlene is a connoisseur of French-language music and is easily the best dressed person at our office.

Dulce Caridad Garcia is a licensed professional counselor who volunteers her skills and services to provide counseling for Spanish-speaking families at Joshua Station. Dulce is fiercely loyal to her community and friends, and enjoys salsa dancing.

Amy Jackson, Mile High Ministries' deputy director, has served survivors of assault and homeless families for over 15 years. She is an avid mountain biker who takes epic rides in the Colorado Rocky Mountains. She is fueled by chocolate.

Nikki Koster loves to spend time with her family, and they know how to have fun. She has been a lacrosse champion as a player and as a coach. Nikki is Justice and Mercy Legal Aid Center's director of development and makes her home in Denver's Baker neighborhood.

Sandy Lee is apprenticeship director at the Issachar Center for Urban Leadership. She is a crisis counselor, social worker and marriage and family therapist—all part of helping students discover who God created them to be. Her thoughts often wander to the beaches of the Bahamas where she was born and raised.

Andy Magel directs the Mile High Workshop. He is a self-professed coffee snob who explores mountains and rivers in Colorado and Wyoming with his wife and son in their cool Westfalia camper van. Ask him about any book Wendell Berry has ever written.

Ryan Taylor AKA Tall Monastic Guy, cultivates his backyard garden where he celebrates abundance with his wife and sons. He is the director of Network and the pastor of St. James Urban Church. Ryan is the wry funny man of our team who earnestly aspires to be a world-renowned yo-yo master.

Steve Thompson founded the Justice and Mercy Legal Aid Center along with Sulma Mendoza. You can usually spot his bright orange Broncos socks, even when he is wearing a suit. Steve got hops—on days his knees will allow it—he enjoys playing pick-up basketball.

End Notes

The Womb of Creation

1. John Burroughs. *Winter Sunshine* (Houghton Mifflin, 1917)
2. T. S. Eliot. *Four Quartets* (Mariner Books, 1968)
3. John 12:24 (RSV)

An Inner Sanctuary

1. Centering Prayer is an ancient way of prayer in the Christian contemplative tradition that was re-introduced to a wider audience in the 20th century by Fr. Thomas Keating, a Trappist monk and priest. An excellent introduction is *Centering Prayer and Inner Awakening* by Cynthia Bourgeault (Cowley Publications, 2012). Many of us make use of the helpful Centering Prayer mobile app available from Contemplative Outreach: www.contemplativeoutreach.org/centering-prayer-mobile-app.

Anything Helps?

1. @FrGregBoyle, June 20, 2018. [Tweet]. https://twitter.com/FrGregBoyle/status/1009549345505415169
2. Two books on this topic that have been especially helpful in our circles: *When Helping Hurts: Alleviating Poverty Without Hurting the Poor... and Yourself* by Brian Fikkert, Steve Corbett (Moody Publishers, 2009). T*oxic Charity: How Churches and Charities Hurt Those They Help, and How to Reverse It*, by Robert Lupton (HarperOne, 2012). Bob Lupton is a friend and fellow community development practitioner at Focused Community Strategies in Atlanta. In in 1992 Bob graciously mentored us in his model for holiday giving—which he called "Dignity for Dads."

Riverside Cemetery

1. Psalm 90:10 (New Life Translation)
2. Belden Lane. *The Solace of Fierce Landscapes* (Oxford University Press, 2007)

Clara Brown and Left Hand

1. Isaiah 58:7
2. Margaret Coel. *Chief Left Hand: Southern Arapaho* (University of Oklahoma Press, 2012)

Liturgy of Sacred Sight

1. First developed during a violent season in Tacoma, Washington, the Liturgy of Sacred Sight ceremony has been adapted by a small international collective called Street Psalms for prayer in neighborhoods from Nairobi to Guatemala City to Camden, New Jersey—and Denver. See page 244 in the Resource section of this book for the complete liturgy.

Be Still Prayer

1. "Be Still" *Our Daily Bread*, February 22, 2016 (https://odb.org/2016/02/22/be-still-3/) September 28, 2018

Viriditas, the Greening

1. Ron Zeilinger, "The Meaning of the Four Directions in Native American Culture." https://www.stjo.org/native-american-culture/native-american-beliefs/four-directions/. July 25, 2018

Generosity

1. Henri Nouwen. *A Spirituality of Fundraising* (Upper Room Books, 2011)

Where Waters Converge

1. https://coralreefwatch.noaa.gov/satellite/education/docs/0_Beginning.pdf. October 15, 2018

Ben Lindsey and Emily Griffith

1. Greg Boyle. *Tattoos on the Heart: The Power of Boundless Compassion* (Free Press, 2011)
2. Nehemiah 2:11-18

Awaking to Grace

1. Bud's Warehouse, "Denver's Favorite Home Improvement Thrift Store," is a social enterprise launched in 1995 by Mile High Ministries. Bud's now thrives as an independent organization that provides job training, and shares warehouse space with Mile High WorkShop.
2. "Twelve Truths I learned from Life and Writing," TED Talk, April 2017 (https://www.ted.com/talks/anne_lamott_12_truths_i_learned_from_life_and_writing/transcript?language=en, accessed 6/21/18)
3. James Finley, our teacher at the Living School for Action and Contemplation; author of *Christian Meditation: Experiencing the Presence of God* (HarperOne, 2005)
4. Anne Lamott, "Twelve Truths I learned from Life and Writing," op. cit.

Ten Days of Prayer

1   Henri Nouwen. *Reaching Out: The Three Movements of the Spiritual Life* (Image, 1986)

Incarnation

1   John 6:38

2   John 15:9

3   John 1:14

4   "The Summer Day," *New and Selected Poems* (Boston: Beacon Press), 1992.

5   Matthew 9:13

6   We are indebted to James Finley, our teacher at the Living School for Action and Contemplation, for insights into the finite and the infinite: "The concrete immediacy of life is the infinite love of God manifesting itself in the present moment." From "Experiencing God's Love" Center for Action and Contemplation website, October 12, 2017 (https://cac.org/experiencing-gods-love-2017-10-12/, retrieved August 24, 2018)

Opening Ourselves to the Word

1   Ruth Haley Barton. *Sacred Rhythms: Arranging Our Lives for Spiritual Transformation* (IVP Books, 2010)

Justice and Shalom

1   Lowell Noble. *From Oppression to Jubilee Justice* (Llumina Press, 2007)

2   Gary Haugen. *Good News About Injustice: A Witness of Courage in a Hurting World* (IVP Books, 2009)

First Residents

1   Simon J. Ortiz. *from Sand Creek* (University of Arizona Pres, 2000)

2   The concept and basic outline for this pilgrimage was borrowed from Stephen J. Leonard's and Thomas J. Noel's book, *A Short History of Denver* (University of Nevada Press, 2016)

3   Ibid.

Carolyn Finnell and Corky Gonzales

1   Virgilio Elizondo, *Galilean Journey: The Mexican-American Promise* (Orbis Books, 2005)

2   1 Corinthians 1:27-28

3   Our colleague Virginia Ortiz contributed invaluable insights in this section, based on her first-person experience with Corky Gonzales in the movement.

From Terror to Strength

1   The National Domestic Violence Hotline. https://www.thehotline.org/resources/statistics/. September 17, 2018

2   National Coalition Against Domestic Violence. https://www.speakcdn.com/assets/2497/colorado.pdf. August 24, 2018

3   Centers for Disease Control and Prevention. Racial and Ethnic Differences in Homicides of Adult Women and the Role of Intimate Partner Violence — United States, 2003–2014. https://www.cdc.gov/mmwr/volumes/66/wr/mm6628a1.htm?s_cid=mm6628a1_w. September 17, 2018

Shaking the System

1   Charles Chaput. "Act Now On Immigration." Editorial in the *Denver Post*, April 18, 2007

Beyond Our Efforts: Transformation

1   Matthew 12:39, 16:4; Luke 11:29

2   John 12:24-26

3   Matthew 12:41 (author paraphrase)

4   George Panichas, ed. *The Simone Weil Reader* (David McKay Co, NY: 1977)

5   Ibid.

6   *The Collected Poems of Theodore Roethke* (Doubleday, 1961).

7   HarperOne, 2014

Letting Go

1   Philippians 4:5-7. Adapted from Gerald Hawthorne, *Philippians* (Word Biblical Commentary, Vol. 43) (Nashville, TN: Word, 1983), 85. Hawthorne argues for this *causative* rendering of the Greek participle huparchon ("existing") for his translation of verse 6, "Precisely because he existed in the form of God," contrary to *concessive* interpretations that result in translations such as "Although he existed in the form of God."

2   Cynthia Bourgeault. T*he Wisdom Jesus: Transforming Heart and Mind—A New Perspective on Christ and His Message* (Shambhala, 2008)

3   Beatrice Bruteau. "Prayer and Identity." *Contemplative Review, 1981*

Trunk or Treat

1 As cited in: https://www.westword.com/news/ending-child-and-family-homelessness-in-colorado-9815037 October 1, 2018

Mapping the Hope of A City

1 Frank Tillapaugh. *Unleashing the Church* (Regal Books, 1985)

2 Ron Sider. *Rich Christians in an Age of Hunger* (IVP Books, 1984)

3 Luis Alberto Urrea. "What Borders Are Really About, and What We Do With Them." *On Being.* https://onbeing.org/programs/luis-alberto-urrea-what-borders-are-really-about-and-what-we-do-with-them-jul2018/. October 30, 2018

A Tale of Two Neighborhoods

1 Phil Goodstein. *Denver from the Bottom Up: A People's History of Early Colorado* (New Social Publications, 2004)

2 https://cloisteredlife.com/directory/denver, November 21, 2018

Langar

1. Walter Brueggemann. *The Prophetic Imagination* (Fortress Press, 2001)

Stirring the Sauce

1 Jazmin's family name has been omitted at her request.

Liberation Ecology

1 English translation: "Come let us worship"

2 James Finley. *Only Love is Real.* Center for Action and Contemplation. https://cac.org/author/james-finley/ October 13, 2017

3 You can keep one pound of carbon pollution out of the atmosphere for each mile of driving you eliminate. Walk, bike, use public transit, and telecommute when you can. Leaving your car at home just two days a week can reduce your greenhouse gas emissions by an average of two tons per year.

Beyond Our Efforts: Christ

1 Colossians 3:11

2 2 Corinthians 11:23-27

3 http://catholic-resources.org/Bible/Joy-Rejoice.htm, October 23, 2018

4 Philippians 3:10-11

5 Philippians 3:21

6 https://www.biblestudytools.com/dictionaries/bakers-evangelical-dictionary/union-with-christ.html, October 23, 2018

7 1 Corinthians 15:21-22

8 2 Corinthians 5:17

9 Ilia Delio, "Revisiting the Franciscan Doctrine of Christ." *Theological Studies* (journal), issue 64, 2003. http://web.sbu.edu/friedsam/ereserve/coughlin_reserve/Delio_4.pdf October 28, 2018

10 Revelation 1:8, 21:6, 22:13

11 Girard Manley Hopkins, "As Kingfishers Catch Fire." *Poems and Prose* (Penguin Classics, 1985)

12 1 Corinthians 13:10-12

13 Daniel Ladinsky, *Love Poems from God: Twelve Sacred Voices from the East and West* (Penguin Books, 2002)